BYE STUDENT LOAN DEBT:

LEARN HOW TO EMPOWER YOURSELF BY ELIMINATING YOUR STUDENT LOANS

Daniel J. Mendelson

BYE Student Loan Debt: Learn How to Empower Yourself by Eliminating Your Student Loans by Daniel J. Mendelson from BYE Student Debt LLC.

Cover & Book Design by Ross Hornish

Executive Editor: Ross Hornish

Grammatical Editor: Charlene Macielag

ISBN: 978-0-9994478-2-6

TABLE OF CONTENTS

ACKNOWLEDGMENTS

I would like to thank my wonderful wife, Meghan, for her patience and stability during our student loan adventure. Despite many nights of anxiety and frustration over our loans and our financial situation, I relied on her determination and composure to help us achieve financial freedom.

I would also like to thank my friend, editor and partner, Ross Hornish, for his passion and creativity in making this book and website a reality.

Lastly, I would like to acknowledge all of our friends and family, as well as our Kickstarter campaign community, for helping to make this vision a reality.

.

PROLOGUE

In the winter of 2011, my personal inspiration for this book struck. I learned that the love of my life had over six figures of student loan debt. She was starting her MBA and entering the professional workforce, holding a bachelor's degree and a master's degree in engineering. Both degrees came at a price. In the process of earning them, she had racked up nearly $120,000 in student loan debt by the age of twenty-three.

In retrospect, she'll be the first to tell you that it was all worth it. At the time though, it was seemingly insurmountable, and she and I were not so sure if the ends justified the means. Fortunately for us, I was one of the lucky ones; I graduated with identical credentials in engineering, but I had only accumulated a mere $10,000 of student loan debt thanks to scholarships and some help from my family. While we earned our MBAs (we both entered the same sponsored MBA program), our interest continued to accrue and our total burden of debt grew to almost $150,000 - essentially the average American mortgage loan, without the house! Not so shockingly, my now wife joined the growing echelons of students saddled with enormous debts after earning their degrees - whether those degrees resulted in successful careers or not. Together we faced the terrifying prospects of a crushing debt situation, with no real end in sight.

Our story of student loan debt is not unique. In 2016, 70% of college graduates exited school with student debt - totaling 43 million student loan borrowers in the United States. All of this debt in the U.S. totals $1.4 trillion dollars in loans, and it is growing at a rate of about $3,000 per second! The average 2017 graduate will leave school with over $37,000 in debt and an average payment of almost $400 per month for 10 years! Of the students that graduate with secondary or professional degrees (such as doctors), more than half have over $100,000 in student loan debt and more than 30% have over $200,000 in debt. Year-after-year, these statistics continue to rise, making a frightening situation for most young professionals trying to start their careers.

If you are one of these graduates in a scary student loan situation, **YOU ARE CLEARLY NOT ALONE**! I wrote this book to share our story of eliminating six figures of student loan debt in five years to help millions of graduates that are in the same situation. This book outlines a simple, detailed strategy that you can use to eradicate your student loan debt: It compiles the lessons we learned and provides solutions for the missteps many graduates take. Following the strategy in the next chapters will change your life and position you for the financial freedom that we now enjoy. Every student loan borrower can achieve this freedom with the right guidance. We are proof.

CHAPTER ONE

ALL ABOUT THAT PAPER(WORK)

Over $100,000 in debt. My wife's alarming debt situation sent me into absolute panic when she first told me. Questions flooded my mind. How did she get into this situation? Does she realize how completely 'screwed' we are? How are we going to get out of this mess? Eventually, I escaped paralysis and came to grips with reality: We needed a solution. My questions became more constructive and less censorious. Does she know the terms of each loan? Who owns her loans? I knew we had to gather as much information as we possibly could. And that, without question, is the first and most important step to breaking free from student loan debt.

We spent an entire weekend digging through her

files. Luckily, she (and her dad) kept everything in one folder ominously labeled "LOANS." Once we had uncovered all of the paper work (and I mean all of the paperwork), I shifted back to complete terror. Her loan situation was much worse than I had anticipated. Even though she had filed away every single document she received over the years, it was impossible to determine who actually owned the student loan debt. The official owner of the loans had changed from the time of loan borrowing to the time of repayment.[1]

Who Owns My Debt?

Getting out of student loan debt means understanding how student loan debt works. The most effective way to garner the knowledge needed to get out of student loan debt is to uncover the information that accompanies each loan. A few hours of due diligence with all of your loans' lenders could save you from a lifetime of devastating debt. Remember, you are not alone here; there are millions of students throughout the world with tens of thousands of dollars of debt[2]. A few hours of effort now will keep you from becoming one of the one in ten student debt holders who are delinquent on their loans and in a tough situation. Most importantly, like

---

[1]   Throughout the Great Recession, student and personal loans were consolidated, sold, bought, and exchanged by a number of large banks as many other banks went out of business. Since then, it has become common practice for loans to be bought and sold by large banking institutions. Unfortunately, this can make life difficult for student loan borrowers with complex loan situations, as the original lenders may not be the current lenders of their loan.

[2]   [http://www.bloomberg.com/news/articles/2015-08-13/borrowers-fall-further-behind-on-1-3-trillion-in-student-loans]

the title implies, it's all about that paper. These few hours will save you money.

Your willingness to pick up this book and learn about your complete student loan situation has the potential to save you thousands of dollars and a lifetime of headaches and fear. It will allow you to say BYE to student loan debt. You can Beat Your Extensive debt in 5 simple steps!   Before you can start to say BYE to your debt – let's review some important definitions that will help you along your journey.

Before you dig into the details, it is important for you to understand the following terms:

Debt Holder – This is the entity that owns your debt. Which bank or institution is backing the loan? Is it a large national bank or a local bank? Is the loan government backed or privately backed? The answers to these questions will allow you to understand the best path towards paying your loans off.

Grace Period – The vast majority of student loans have a grace period. A grace period is a set amount of time between when you graduate and when you must begin paying back your student loans. Grace periods range in duration, but generally last less than one year and most commonly six months. Ensure you note the presence and length of each student loan's grace period so that you do not get penalized for missing payments.

Principle – The original loan amount that was borrowed, excluding interest.

Unpaid/Accrued Interest – The amount of interest

that has accrued on the loan, but has yet to be paid. If you have a Subsidized Stafford Loan (see below), you will not have any accrued interest. Otherwise, you will be accruing additional debt based on your interest rate if you are not actively paying down your debt.

Interest & Interest Rates – Interest is simply the amount of money a lender charges a borrower, as a percentage of your total loan, on a monthly and annual basis to have a loan. It is the charge from the government or bank for providing a loan (there is no free money)! While many people often ignore this term, it can be the most important aspect of your student loan; it is often the case that students end up paying just as much or more than their principle amount in interest. If this is left unchecked, people can become smothered by their debt quickly. A higher interest rate is often charged to riskier loans where the borrower is seen to have a higher risk of defaulting on their loan. Students with no job or income and large amounts of debt precisely fit this profile. This will be the subject of your action plan in later chapters, but for now, differentiate as to whether your loan has a FIXED or VARIABLE rate.

A fixed loan - means that you pay a constant interest rate for the life of the loan. For example, you may pay an interest rate of 6.5% for 10 years.

A variable loan's interest rate fluctuates with the national interest rates. For example, this may mean that one year you'll pay 5% interest on your loan, while the following year you'll pay a higher rate if the national interest rates rise. Likewise, your interest rate will decrease if the national interest rate falls. They usually have an upper limit in the high teens and a lower limit in the low single digits.

Compound vs. Simple Interest – A simple interest loan accumulates interest on only the original principle amount for the loan. A compound interest rate is paid on the principle of the loan AND all previously accrued interest. Compound interest is the most common type of loan and it is the reason why debt can balloon out of control if left unchecked.

Types of Loans:

Subsidized – calendar with $1000 at the beginning of the month, $1000 at the end Unsubsidized

Federal Subsidized Stafford Loan – This type of loan is subsidized by the government. All interest is forgiven while a student is in school and for the grace period after graduation. After the grace period, interest will start to accrue like a normal loan.

Federal Unsubsidized Stafford Loan – Unlike the loan above, the student borrower accrues interest from the moment he or she accepts the student loan. Students are not responsible for paying this interest while they are in school or during the grace period, but it continues to add up and it will have to be paid after the grace period ends.

Private Loans – These loans are usually only sought out when a student has maximized his or her loan allowances for Stafford Loans. Private loans generally carry higher interest rates and less favorable terms for young adults. It is very common for students with large amounts of loans to require these additional private loans for uncovered tuition and living expenses.

General Loan Terms – These are the rules that govern your loan and dictate how it should be paid back. Read the terms carefully so that your path to financial freedom is not hindered. The terms will help you to determine your minimum monthly payments and the due dates of the loan payments. Missing payments often result in negative marks against your credit, so the stakes are high.

Specifically, the general loan terms will help you answer questions such as:

- When do I have to start making my initial loan payments?

- How quickly must I pay the loan back to avoid penalties?

- Does my loan have any advanced payment penalties? (Yes, you can incur more costs for paying your loans back too quickly in rare scenarios!)

So, is there any good news?

A highly misunderstood concept is 'good' debt versus 'bad' debt. In general, lower interest loans that serve a valuable purpose, such as a mortgage on a house, are considered good debt. Conversely, higher interest loans on purchases that do not provide value, such as credit card debt, are considered bad debt. Student loans are a form of good debt – believe it or not! Why? Your student loan is providing you with the value of education, which will result in you obtaining a higher paying job than if you had not received a college degree (hopefully!). However, mismanaged student loans can quickly turn into a form of bad debt if the principles outlined in this book are not followed. Additionally, student loans can be a form of bad debt if you take a large student loan and do not increase your earning potential. For example, let's say you could earn $30,000 a year without a college education, but you go to an expensive college and get into $150,000 of debt. After college, your salary is $35,000 with limited increased earning potential. This may now be a form of bad debt, as you made a large investment that has had a very limited effect on your overall earning potential.

While many of you reading this book have already finished your college education, it is important for younger friends and family members to keep this in mind as they make their secondary education decisions. We will address these decisions and many others in Chapter 8 of this book titled, "Hindsight is 20/20."

The above information is required to be successful in paying off your student loans in a quick and efficient manner. Let's go over the example below. This example illustrates the dangers of what happens when someone does not understand the concepts we discussed so far and does not follow the principles outlined in this book.

Let's assume you are a student loan debt holder and you have approximately $26,500 of debt (LESS than the average student loan debt in the United States) and are paying a 6.5% fixed interest rate for the life of the thirty-year loan. If you were to make the minimum payments for this entire loan, your repayments would look like the following:

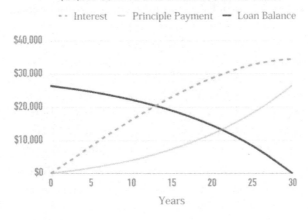

$26,500 LOAN AT 6.5% INTEREST FOR 30 YEARS

PRINCIPLE REPAYMENT CHART

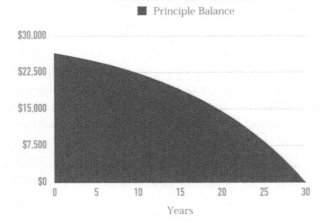

In this scenario, you would end up paying $56,500 in total payments, or more than double the original

$26,500 principle, due to $30,000 in interest payments! This is a very realistic picture of the situation YOU might be in and it is an illustration that represents why millions of Americans end up drowning in debt over their lifetimes. It is why many student debt holders have a feeling that there is no end in sight and it is why one in ten end up in delinquency.

However, with the proper knowledge about each and every detail of your loan paired with reasonable goals, you can overcome this challenge by paying your debt off with more favorable terms, less interest, and, most importantly, more SPEED! Once you have finished discovering all of the details of your loans, you should create a very simple Excel chart (or the calculator tools linked to this book) that will allow you to completely understand the terms of each loan, set goals, and reign in your debt. Once you finish a few hours on the phone with banks, activate online accounts (Do you remember all the passwords you or your parents created over four years ago?), pore over the stacks of paperwork, and assemble all of the pertinent information, you should be left with the a simple table that looks like the table below. Use the interactive calculator tools of this book's accompanying website http://student.byeloandebt.com/ to input your personal loan situation and get outputs such as the table below. For each step in this book's process, you will see hyperlinks to tools that will allow you to have an organized and personalized snapshot of your loan situation and goals, which can be used to employ the plan outlined in this book.

OUR LOAN SITUATION					
LOAN SOURCE	PRINCIPLE	UNPAID INTEREST	TOTAL DEBT	IR (%)	FIX. OR VAR.
ACS	$7,090	$1,867	$8,961	6.8	FIX
FED STAFF	$5,500	-	$5,500	6.00	FIX
FED STAFF	$5,500	-	$5,500	5.60	FIX
FED UNSUB STAFF	$2,000	$318	$2,318	6.80	FIX
GREAT LAKES	$17,887	$2,617	$20,504	3.58	FIX
WELLS FARGO	$7,142	-	$7,142	10.7	VAR
WELLS FARGO	$17,167	-	$17,167	8.25	VAR
DIRECT SUBS STAFF	$8,500	-	$8,500	6.80	FIX
DIRECT UNSUB STAFF	$12,000	$1,069	$13,069	6.80	FIX
DIRECT SUBS STAFF	$8,500	-	$8,500	6.80	FIX
DIRECT UNSUBS STAFF	$10,602	$246	$10,848	6.80	FIX
CAR LOAN	$6,768	-	$6,768	6.94	FIX
TOTAL	**$108,660**	**$6,119**	**$114,779**	7.02	

Access calculator tools at:
http://student.byeloandebt.com/calculators/

When I completed this activity for my wife, she had over $110,000 of loans at an average interest rate of over 7%! And this total didn't include another

$10,000 of my own student loans and the future interest she was going to accumulate as we earned MBAs!

After assembling this information, you will likely want to do what I did: Pour a stiff drink and forget about it all together. However, when you wake up from your stupor, hopefully you will begin to feel a calming sense of empowerment. Why? You now have the knowledge to control and correct your student loan debt situation. This is the first step to effectively managing your student loans and gaining financial freedom. Say BYE and Beat Your Extensive debt!

Key Takeaways:

- Learn the basic definitions outlined in this chapter

- Create a simple table or use our online calculator tools to outline all loan sources, principles, unpaid interest, interest rates, and general loan terms such as fixed vs. variable interest payments

5 STEPS TO GET RID OF YOUR STUDENT LOANS

STEP 01	STEP 02	STEP 03	STEP 04	STEP 05
ASSESS YOUR SITUATION	CREATE A BUDGET	SET A GOAL	RESTRUCTURE & REFINANCE	EXECUTE, MANAGE & ADJUST

CHAPTER TWO

BALLIN' ON A BUDGET REQUIRES A PLAN

Take a deep breath. Some of the hardest work is now over. Now that you have established the conditions of all of your loans, you are well on your way to beginning the process of eradicating debt. As a wise man once said, "Knowledge is power." And, although this knowledge may be terrifying and monotonous, it will put you on the path to success with your debt.[3]

The next step is to create that mysterious thing that your parents have been telling you about for years – a

---

[3] This chapter and the vast majority of this book assumes that you are in the process or have finished getting your degree, and that you are essentially stuck with the loans you have. Avoiding debt in the first place is the focus of the last chapter "Hindsight is 20/20." There are numerous options, such as military service and Teach for America that provide loan forgiveness programs and/or contribute to the down payment of loans. Assuming these are not realistic options for you at this point, you will have to alleviate your debt the old fashion way!

BUDGET. Before you can set your goals and put an action plan in place, you need to not only assess your loan situation, but you must also assess your personal financial situation. Below is an example of a simplified budget that a typical graduate might create. Remember that you can always access our website tools to create a similar budget tailored to your financial situation.

The budget below assumes an annual income of $50,000, a modest income from additional side jobs, 401k contributions (a subject that deserves another book of its own), and 'average' expenses for daily living and activities.

MONTHLY INCOME	$4,167
OTHER (TUTORING, COACHING, ETC.)	$100
TOTAL MONTHLY INCOME	**$4,267**
401K CONTRIBUTION	$250
TAXES	$750
CAR LOAN	$200
CAR INSURANCE	$100
BASIC LIVING EXPENSES (RENT, UTILITIES, GAS, ETC.)	$1,500
OTHER (ENTERTAINMENT, TRAVEL, ETC.)	$300
TOTAL MONTHLY EXPENSES	**$3,100**
MONTHLY NET	**$1,167**

Access tools at: http://student.byeloandebt.com/calculators/

If your situation is drastically different than the one presented above and you're netting much less than $1,000 a month, have no fear. Surprisingly, the chart above is nearly identical to the COMBINED income and expenses of my wife and I while we earned our MBAs (full-time) and worked (part-time). With a combined monthly savings (net) of about $1,200 and a debt of over $120,000, it's no wonder that the numbers overwhelmed us. The important part, though, is that we didn't allow the numbers to overcome us. After collecting the information on our student loans, creating a budget was our second step to becoming financially free.

Obviously your personal situation might vary significantly from the scenario above, but it is easy to recreate this budget with your personal sources of income and expenses. The first place to start is with your weekly, bi-weekly or monthly paychecks, adding in any other income that you accrue through side jobs, and your monthly bills. We will outline this process below.

As a side note, if your financial health is in a precarious situation, it is highly recommended that you find a way to supplement your income. For example, my wife and I have specialized knowledge in specific academic and professional areas that cost us a fortune in student loans. Why not put that knowledge to work? Whenever we had the bandwidth, we charged $40 per hour to tutor high school and undergraduate students through their studies. I also turned one of my personal interests into a side job. Growing up, I was a soccer player. Having a love for the game, I decided to become a licensed soccer referee, which paid me $30-$50 per hour on weekends – and I got to participate in a sport I enjoyed! In the age of the sharing economy, part time jobs can provide large supplemental income with relative ease, such as Uber or Lyft driving.

While second jobs can be burdensome, eat into your personal time, and be downright tiring, these efforts will make a monumental difference by increasing your disposable income; and this income can be used towards paying off your loans. This difference, which I will show you in the following chapters and in the below example, can result in loans being paid off years in advance, with thousands of dollars in savings.

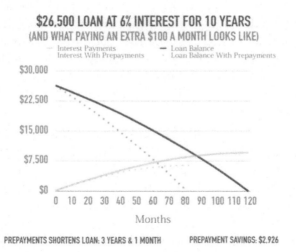

$26,500 LOAN AT 6% INTEREST FOR 10 YEARS
(AND WHAT PAYING AN EXTRA $100 A MONTH LOOKS LIKE)

— Interest Payments
Interest With Prepayments

— Loan Balance
Loan Balance With Prepayments

Months

PREPAYMENTS SHORTENS LOAN: 3 YEARS & 1 MONTH   PREPAYMENT SAVINGS: $2,926

The example above shows a loan of $26,000 with a 6% interest rate over a ten-year period. If this was your student loan and you paid $100 extra per month in payments, you would reduce your loan by three years and save nearly $3,000! This illustrates how aggressively paying off paralyzing student loans with a little extra money on the side can make a huge difference over the life of a loan.

So, in essence, don't be fooled; just because a loan has a minimum payment doesn't mean that this amount is all you should contribute to your loans. We will continue to demonstrate why you should always pay more than the minimum, barring a few rare exceptions, as we progress through this book.

Ready to create a budget? Now that you understand the importance of creating one, the next step is to outline each of your expenses. The easiest way to do this is to take the last three months of bank statements, credit card statements, and any other outlays, and compile these together. In general, it is best practice to include your average spend over the last three months, excluding one-time or abnormal purchases. This will allow you to estimate basic living expenses, such as rent and utilities, entertainment, and any other recurring, monthly spending. Additionally, you can determine your average tax burden based on the average amount of money withheld from your paychecks (assuming you filed your W-4 withholdings correctly). Lastly, make sure to include monthly expenses like 401k contributions[4], taxes and health care expenses that might get deducted from your regular paycheck. This will lead you to a table that is tailored to your personal financial situation. This is what you are left with:

---

[4]   Many companies offer 401k benefit programs, in which they match tax-free contributions. These contributions are investments that have a lifetime to grow into a retirement 'nest egg.' We will explore more about personal trade-off decisions with respect to savings versus loan payments later in the book. However, if you have the ability to contribute towards these benefits, do it! This is free money that your company provides for those who take advantage of the matching programs. Do not leave this money on the table!

TOTAL INCOME – TOTAL EXPENSES = MONTHLY NET INCOME

This monthly net income number is the total amount of money you have leftover for life events (Be prepared for the inevitable wedding invites and baby showers!), travel, entertainment, and, of course, your student loans! You have two simple ways to increase this number so that you can ultimately pay more towards your student loans: increase your income by changing and/or adding jobs OR decrease your monthly expenses. There are a host of cost-cutting methods to decrease your monthly expenses, but examples include downsizing, eliminating cable TV, and carpooling to work.

Now that you have a complete picture of your student loan situation and your monthly net income, you have one last step to complete before you are ready to execute your plan to eliminate debt: set a goal. Without a clear goal you will be less likely to stick with a plan and achieve it. How can you decide on a goal? Here is a list of questions to ask yourself that may help you identify a target:

- How long do I want to have student loans?

- How fast can I reasonably eliminate these loans and still live my life in a manner suitable to my needs?

- What future life events will I need to pay for in the next one, three, five, ten, twenty-plus years, and how will my student loan debt affect my ability to pay for these events?

- When do I want to retire and how will these loans affect that goal? (Yes, it is NEVER too early to start thinking about retirement)

With this type of personal reflection, you will be driven to your goal. My goal at this stage was extremely simple: eliminate the six figures of student loan debt that my wife and I had accrued, in five years. It was an aggressive goal, but one that we both wanted to achieve in order to enjoy our prime years without worrying about student loan debt.

For my wife and I, at that time, our next five years included one more year of studying for our MBAs and four years of full-time employment. Your goal will likely vary compared to our goal based on your personal financial situation, but this was our target.

Our original goal when we began this process was incredibly aggressive; we aimed to eliminate our debt within three years. To see what we would have had to pay on a monthly and yearly basis, I created a simple amortization table. An amortization table is a fancy way of describing a loan payment schedule. This table showed me how much these monthly payments would be to have a year-end balance of $0 after three years, assuming $130,000 of debt, including interest. This calculation assumed that the average interest rate of all of our loans would be constant. Below is what this looked like:

YEAR	BALANCE	YEARLY PAY.	INT. PAY.	PRIN. PAY.	END BALANCE
1	$130,000	$49,545	$9,113	$40,432	$89,567
2	$89,567	$49,545	$6,278	$43,267	$46,300
3	$46,300	$49,545	$3,245	$46,300	-

This amortization table showed us that we needed to make $49,545 in payments annually, or over $4,000 per month in order to pay off these loans in three years. That plan quickly faded away as we barely made that much together as students at the time, excluding expenses – and likely, it would have been impossible to successfully execute this plan without a large windfall of money from a distant and wealthy relative. This exercise alone shed light on how difficult this process was going to be. **If we wanted to be successful, we knew we had to be realistic**. In the end, we remained as aggressive as possible, but we adjusted our goal to a five-year plan, as you will see below:

YEAR	BALANCE	YEARLY PAY.	INT. PAY.	PRIN. PAY.	END BALANCE
1	$130,000	$31,714	$9,113	$22,601	$107,398.72
2	$107,398	$31,714	$7,528	$24,185	$83,213.09
3	$83,213	$31,714	$5,833	$25,881	$57,332.05
4	$57,332	$31,714	$4,018	$27,695	$29,636.74
5	$29,636	$31,714	$2,077	$29,636	-

Notice that the overall yearly payment is the sum of the interest paid and the principle paid. The 'principle payment' represents the amount of the original loan that you are paying off, while interest is the amount of money that has accrued given the percentage that the loaner charges for providing this loan. Notice how interest payments are very high in the early years and lessen over time as the loan becomes smaller. This is extremely important. This is the reason that you always want to try and get the lowest interest rate possible on student/private loans. We will be exploring this further in the next chapter.

To understand this concept more fully, imagine that you are eating a rib eye steak. The meat represents the principle and the fat represents the interest. In order to get to the good stuff (the principle), you have to trim around the fat (pay off the interest). Interest works the same way, but unlike the fat in steak, the interest will continue to expand and multiply should the principle remain untouched.

Are you ready to get to the good meat? Make sure to input your personal information and goals into our calculator tools at http://student.byeloandebt.com to have this information automatically calculated and displayed like the chart above!

Even after my wife and I adjusted our goal from three to five years, we still needed over $31,000 in payments annually, or $2,580 monthly. Instantly, we knew that if this was going to be possible, we both needed to land decent jobs and supplement them with work on the side. It also became clear to us that we would need to dramatically cut back on spending to earn a monthly net income of OVER $2,580. Notice how I said OVER; we had major life events planned for the future, such as buying a house and taking yearly vacations to spend time together. We didn't want to choose debt over our lives, so we budgeted slightly over our monthly loan payment requirement. This forced us to make the hard decisions on which expenses to cut and on how many additional hours we could work per week to supplement our income.

For us, we were lucky. We found a balance that would allow us to meet our goals and still live (somewhat) comfortably. What about you? If you're just not making enough to meet your goal, then this next section is for you.

If you have maxed out your net income and you are still not able to meet your student loan goals, the only other option is to force the terms of your loan to be more favorable (if possible) so that your loan payments are smaller and can be paid off quicker. This is the next piece of the puzzle for you to execute on a student loan elimination plan.

The information gathering and budgeting is now complete. It is time to roll up your sleeves to begin the hard work of executing your plan and saying **BYE** to **B**eat **Y**our **E**xtensive debt!

Key Takeaways:

- Monthly net income = Monthly income – monthly expenses

- Determine your monthly net income through a simple budget

- Use the amortization tool outlined in this chapter to set your BYE goals and understand the monthly payment required to meet those goals

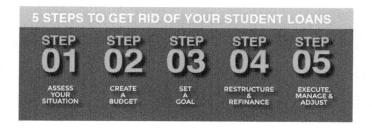

5 STEPS TO GET RID OF YOUR STUDENT LOANS

STEP 01	STEP 02	STEP 03	STEP 04	STEP 05
ASSESS YOUR SITUATION	CREATE A BUDGET	SET A GOAL	RESTRUCTURE & REFINANCE	EXECUTE, MANAGE & ADJUST

CHAPTER THREE

BARGAIN HUNTING

For those of you that are nearing graduation or have recently completed your studies, you are likely to have a million things going on in your head right now. How do I find a job? Is the current job I am choosing the right one? What is the real world going to be like?

However, one of the most important questions you need to be asking yourself is, "What is my current loan situation and when do I need to actually start making payments?" The grace period for most loans is six months. Trust me when I tell you that these six months will come quicker than you can ever imagine. Time simply goes quicker as serious responsibilities and obligations stack up. You will be transitioning your entire life to focus on your career in the scary 'real world,' but you must not get distracted and forget to keep a pulse on the goals you set in order to eradicate your debt. When I graduated, I hated it when people kept saying, "Welcome to the real world," as if I was living in a fantasy world before I graduated college. However, your life truly does change. Whether you just graduated or not, NOW is the time to get a full grasp of your loan situation as described in the first two chapters. It is never too early or too late to start!

So, now that you know everything about your loans and you (hopefully) have a job, what happens next? The first thing to do is go back to the very first chart you put together using the BYE website's online calculator tools. It should look similar to something like this:

LOAN SOURCE	PRINCIPLE	UNPAID INT.	TOTAL DEBT	IR (%)	FIX OR VAR
ACS	$7,090.00	$1,867.00	$8,961	6.80	FIX
FED STAFF	$5,500.00	-	$5,500	6.00	FIX
FED STAFF	$5,500.00	-	$5,500	5.60	FIX
FED UNSUB STAFF	$2,000.00	$318.82	$2,318	6.80	FIX
GREAT LAKES	$17,887.00	$2,617.17	$20,504	3.58	FIX
WELLS FARGO	$7,142.00	-	$7,142	10.7	VAR
WELLS FARGO	$17,167.00	-	$17,167	8.25	VAR
DIRECT SUBS STAFF	$8,500.00	-	$8,500	6.80	FIX
RRDIRECT UNSUB STAFF	$12,000.00	$1,069.34	$13,069	6.80	FIX
DIRECT SUBS STAFF	$8,500.00	-	$8,500	6.80	FIX
DIRECT UNSUBS STAFF	$10,602.00	$246.56	$10,848	6.80	FIX
CAR LOAN	$6,768	-	$6,768	6.94	FIX
TOTAL	$108,660	$6,118.89	$114,778	7.02	

The goal now is to sort through each loan, one by one, and to get the most favorable terms possible for each loan. The very first thing I did - which I suggest you do as well - was consolidate all loans from the same lender into a single loan and set up automatic payments. This will ensure that you do not miss payments, which could have a severe negative effect on your credit. But even more importantly, by setting up automatic payments, you may also receive a slight discount on the interest rate you pay for each loan. For example, the federal government gives you a 0.25% interest rate break if you consolidate all federal loans from the same loan servicer and set up automatic payments.

In our situation, we consolidated and set automatic payments on:

- All of my wife's federally owned government loans totaling about $55,000 at 6.8% interest

- All of my federally owned government loans ($10,000 not shown above) at 6.8% interest

- Her two Wells Fargo loans, which were personal loans needed above and beyond federal loans, totaling about $33,000 (including interest) at over 9% interest

- Her Great Lakes loan totaling $20,000 at 3.58% interest

- Her ACS loan, which was also a federally owned government student loan bought by ACS, totaling $9,000 at 6.8% interest

Each of these loans provides a great learning experience and a tactic you can use to help set you off on the right path for success with your loans.

Federal Government Loans:

We consolidated all of our loans that were owned by the federal government and set up automatic payments on the loans. Simply by setting up automatic payments on the account, we each received a 0.25% rate reduction (this is common). The interest rates on our federal government loans dropped from 6.8% to 6.55%. While this might not sound like a big deal, remember that small adjustments in interest rates can make a difference of thousands of dollars in interest paid towards a loan.

30 YEAR LOAN – 6.8% INTEREST RATE

Loan Amount	Interest Rate	Terms of Loan
$60,000	6.8%	30 Yr. Fixed

Monthly Payment	Total Paid Towards Loan	Total Interest Paid
$391.16	$140,815.84	$80,815.84

30 YEAR LOAN - 6.55% INTEREST RATE

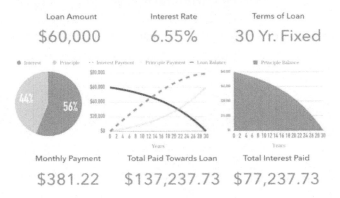

Loan Amount	Interest Rate	Terms of Loan
$60,000	6.55%	30 Yr. Fixed

Monthly Payment	Total Paid Towards Loan	Total Interest Paid
$381.22	$137,237.73	$77,237.73

How big of a difference can 0.25% make? For a thirty-year loan of $60,000, this tiny adjustment in interest would make a difference of $3,000 paid over the lifetime of the loan. This is $3,000 extra that could be used to pay off other loans, invest in a house, or invest for retirement.

As you can see, this rate reduction is essentially free money that the federal government is giving you. The rate reduction serves as an incentive for millions of students to set up automatic payments so that they are less likely to miss payments or worse - default on their loans. Why would the government do this?

The government, like most private banks, will do this because it helps them! You better believe that Uncle Sam and all other banking institutions are going to get their money back some way, somehow. Millions of American students end up missing payments or defaulting on their loans. By giving up a small interest rate now, this significantly increases the chances that graduates will pay on time, as they will be automatically enrolled to pay via monthly bills and direct deposit. In the end, the government gives up a little bit of money to save a lot of time and money in collecting loan payments. Make sure you take advantage of this incentive.[5]

For my wife and I, this exercise placed our federal government loans on cruise control in terms of payment management. However, we were not done yet – there is more to come on federal student loans.

Private Loans:

When looking into our loan situation, the largest pain point was around my wife's private loans. She had two private loans with the following interest rates:

- $20,000 from Great Lakes at 3.58% interest
- $24,000 from Wells Fargo at a combined interest rate of over 9%!

The Great Lakes loan of 3.58% is a superb interest rate on a student loan in today's environment, meaning there was very little chance we could get a better interest rate. We left that one alone and set up automatic payments.

---

[5] The other important note about federal government interest rates is that for most of the late-2000s to today, the federal government has charged students 6.5%+ interest for their loans. By comparison, in 2016 and 2017, most private and federal loans are in the 3.5-5.5% range. Since Uncle Sam is charging a large premium to the American student compared to a normal loan, the government can afford to incentivize these same students to setup automatic payments and slightly reduce its interest rate.

The biggest concern came from the Wells Fargo loan with over 9% interest. That was a crushing interest rate; at the time, it was nearly three times the national interest rates. She was paying over $2,000 a year in interest alone, just for having ownership of the loan. To put that into perspective, do you remember the $3,000 in savings that resulted from the interest rate reduction of 0.25% in the Federal Government Loans section above? Well if that same loan was 9%, the borrower would end up paying over $35,000 more towards that exact same $60,000 loan over the same thirty-year period of time, all because of this outrageously high interest rate.

30 YEAR LOAN - 9% INTEREST RATE

Loan Amount	Interest Rate	Terms of Loan
$60,000	9%	30 Yr. Fixed

Monthly Payment	Total Paid Towards Loan	Total Interest Paid
$482.77	$173,798.49	$113,798.49

After a little digging, I found out why my wife had been given such a high interest rate: She already had nearly six figures of debt when she needed to get this private loan; She was entering graduate/professional school and not making a significant amount of income; She had no credit history; and, she had no cosigner[6] on the loan. From the perspective of Wells Fargo, this was an EXTREMELY risky loan, and she fit the profile of someone that had a high chance of defaulting on his or her loan. Unfortunately (but understandably), this is why Wells Fargo charged her a high premium in the form of an interest rate.

Hopefully you are starting to recognize that interest rates, if left unchecked, can ravage your financial future. So how did we fix this astronomical interest rate? The answer to this problem is a wonderful tool called loan consolidation. If you are a graduate, you probably get inundated with loan consolidation offers, and it is likely that most do not have great terms. However, this beautiful tool can save you tens of thousands of dollars in interest rates if you know how to use it right.

Most local and national banks and credit unions offer some sort of loan consolidation program, where one organization will purchase your loans, from one or multiple sources, and consolidate the loans into one simple payment. To start, I would recommend shopping around at your local or national bank and a variety of competitors for rates on the loans you would like to reduce. Additionally, there are newer

---

[6]   Co-signing is an important feature of private loans. From the example above, you can see that my wife got nearly double the interest rate on her loan compared to if she had a cosigner backing her loan. A cosigner is simply a family member or friend who has an established credit line and is willing to sign up to pay your debt should you default on your loan. For the bank, a co-signer is essentially an insurance policy for people that may default on their loans in the future. If this were to occur, the co-signer would be legally responsible for 100% of the remaining balance of a loan. It is highly recommended that you find a trusted person to co-sign on your loans so that you receive the best possible interest rate. Then, ensure that you do not default so that the co-signer is not left with your debt!

online banks that offer creative loan programs for student graduates. By providing all of your loan information, these banks will be able to give you a rate quote WITHOUT running your credit report. It is important that potential lenders do not run your credit until you are confident about the bank you would like to choose. Why? Multiple credit checks can actually hurt your credit, which can reduce your chance of getting a lower interest rate. In order for banks to provide you with an interest rate estimate, they will likely need all loan information (which you should have collected by now), estimated income, personal information and an estimated credit score. A credit score can be found online through a number of online sources that allow you to check your credit at least once a year for free without any affect to your credit score.

In our situation, we chose to consolidate only the following loan (as the existing Great Lakes loan already had a phenomenal rate):

- $24,000 from Wells Fargo at a combined interest rate of over 9%!

This left us with about $34,000 in loans at a sky high interest rate that would cost us tens of thousands of dollars over the life of the loan if we couldn't reduce the interest rate. After shopping this loan at five banks, we found that Wells Fargo (go figure!) had the best loan consolidation program for our current financial situation. At this stage, we were both gainfully employed and had built credit through multiple sources. This made us appear significantly less risky in the bank's eyes as opposed to when my wife originally received the loan. It is important to note, you do not have to have a well-established history or career to utilize these programs. Often, proof of sufficient income to cover the loan or the ability to procure a co-signer will allow you to effectively utilize these consolidation programs.

Wells Fargo gave us two options:

- A variable interest loan at 3.75% over five years
- A fixed interest loan at 6.24% over five years

Most likely, you will receive similar options for a fixed interest rate versus variable interest rate. The choice you make will be highly dependent upon your situation and your goals. In both cases, it is crucial that you read the fine print to ensure that you will not be penalized for early payments and that you are aware of any other terms that could interfere with your loan repayment goals. Since the 2008 financial crash, banks are required to be much more transparent with their financial transactions. However, taking an hour to read the fine print may save you many headaches in the long run.

Fixed Vs. Variable Interest Rates

For a fixed interest loan, you will pay a higher interest rate, as you are locking in that interest rate for the life of the loan. The advantage to accepting a fixed interest rate is that it does not fluctuate as national interest rates change in the years to come. For a student loan borrower that plans to pay back his or her loan over a long period of time, a fixed interest loan is in the student's best interests as he or she will be protected from the risk of interest rates increasing over time.

Variable interest rates are just as the name suggests: variable. They include a minimum interest rate PLUS another interest rate that is added on top; the latter interest rate is based on current market interest rates. The initial rate the bank quotes you reflects the rate that the bank will charge at the beginning term of the loan. However, if interest rates go up, you will have a higher interest rate; if interest rates go down, you will have lower interest rates. The interest rate you pay will never go below the minimum or above an outrageously high maximum (usually 15-20%). This type of loan is best suited for someone who has a shorter time horizon to loan repayment.

My wife and I chose a variable interest loan, as our goal was to eliminate this loan within an aggressive five-year time period. Over such a short period of time, it was unlikely that interest rates would spike so high that the rates would become detrimental to our goals. It was a calculated risk, but it was one that we felt informed enough to take.

There are many student borrowers, however, that go astray with variable interest loans. While a student may lock in a low interest rate on a ten-year loan, there is nothing to stop the variable interest rate from ballooning over the years if national interest rates rise over that period of time. This puts the borrower in a situation where all of his or her budgeted payments go towards interest, rather than towards the actual principle of the loan. This will undoubtedly extend the life of the loan and therefore increase the amount of money the student pays for the loan for many years to come.

What can you do to prevent from falling into a variable interest rate trap? Be sure to look into the financial horizon of the global marketplace during your repayment period, as this will affect the variable interest rate. At the time of writing this book (2016), interest rates are near the lowest levels in the history of the United States. Consequently, it is expected that interest rates will rise over the next five years (at least marginally).

About a year after going through this exercise with our private loans, I started investigating federally owned student loans in greater detail. After we successfully lowered the interest rates on our private loans, I became frustrated that we could not similarly consolidate our federally owned loans and lower our interest rates; after all, we were stuck with 6.8% interest rates on over $50,000 of debt from these loans!

Finally, after hours of research, I found that the act of consolidating federally owned loans was not previously allowed due to restrictions imposed by the federal government. However, new laws and regulations provide an opportunity to consolidate federal loans with private companies. It is extremely important for you to understand that there are many benefits you will give up if you decide to consolidate a federally owned government loan into a privately owned loan. The benefits you may forfeit include the following:

- Lower-income monthly payment plans that are more flexible for lower-income, new graduates
- Federal forgiveness programs that can be

utilized by working for certain federal, not-for-profit programs, such as Teach for America
- Favorable forbearance programs
- A longer repayment time horizon than most private loans

If you plan to utilize any of the above, do NOT refinance your federal loan into a private loan. This section of the book is not for you.

So, is this decision right for you? If you have a much shorter and aggressive loan repayment time horizon and you are confident in your ability to repay your loans quickly, this may be your best option. By consolidating your federal loans into private loans, you will most likely receive a lower interest rate.

For consolidation of our federal loans, we shopped many new online student loan companies and found that SOFI was the best for our financial situation. Because we lived in the state of Tennessee, we were unable to apply for a variable interest rate loan due to state laws, unfortunately. (These types of loans are dependent on local and state regulations.) Instead, we ended up with a fixed interest rate loan. In the end, we reduced our federal loan interest rates from 6.8% to 5.3% - a WHOPPING 1.5%. We also had a new five-year payback period, as opposed to our previous twenty-five year maximum term from the federal government.

Over the course of the first year of our five-year plan (while we continued to research and consolidate our loans with the highest interest rates), I was able to pay off my entire student loan debt of $10,000 by cutting expenses and, somewhat begrudgingly, handing over my first year's bonus to the creditors. In addition, my wife paid off her car from a loan originating in 2008. Her loan student loan situation was simplified from this:

LOAN SOURCE	PRINC.	UNPAID INTEREST	TOTAL DEBT	IR (%)	FIX OR VAR
ACS	$7,090.00	$1,867.00	$8,961	6.80%	FIX
FED STAFF	$5,500.00	-	$5,500	6.00%	FIX
FED STAFF	$5,500.00	-	$5,500	5.60%	FIX
FED UNSUB STAFF	$2,000.00	$318.82	$2,318	6.80%	FIX
GREAT LAKES	$17,887.00	$2,617.17	$20,504	3.58%	FIX
WELLS FARGO	$7,142.00	-	$7,142	10.74%	VAR
WELLS FARGO	$17,167.00	-	$17,167	8.25%	VAR
DIRECT SUBS STAFF	$8,500.00	-	$8,500	6.80%	FIX
RRDIRECT UNSUB STAFF	$12,000.00	$1,069.34	$13,069	6.80%	FIX
DIRECT SUBS STAFF	$8,500.00	-	$8,500	6.80%	FIX
DIRECT UNSUBS STAFF	$10,602.00	$246.56	$10,848	6.80%	FIX
CAR LOAN	$6,768	-	$6,768	6.94%	FIX
TOTAL	$108,660	$6,118.89	$114,778	7.02%	

To this:

LOAN SOURCE	TOTAL DEBT	IR (%)	FIXED OR VARIABLE
SOFI	$55,000.00	5.38%	FIXED
GREAT LAKES	$23,000	3.58%	FIXED
WELLS FARGO	$33,929.00	3.75%	VARIABLE
TOTAL	$111,929.00	4.51%	

After months of rate shopping and consolidation, this was our new and improved loan situation. Quite a change from the original, scary chart with twelve different loans! Notice that the overall debt level did not change significantly; her loans continued to accrue interest. As students, we were only able to pay off my $10,000 loan, small amounts of her interest, and her car loan. However we were able to consolidate her student loans from more than ten payments down to three, and we were also able to reduce the overall interest rate from over 7% to 4.5%!

Two and a half percent may not seem like a significant drop at first glance. However, with nearly $120,000 in debt, this interest rate reduction yielded a huge savings for my wife and I. In fact, had we repaid our loans over a ten-year period, this 2.5% interest drop would have resulted in our scheduled payments decreasing by $150 per month. That equates to a total savings of about $18,000 over the lifespan of the loan; that's over 10% of our entire debt – all without making any additional or accelerated payments! The two charts below show this phenomenon. By keeping everything else equal and making minimum loan payments on a ten year loan, the total payments reduce from \$167,000 to \$149,000 when you reduce interest payments from 7% to 4.5%.

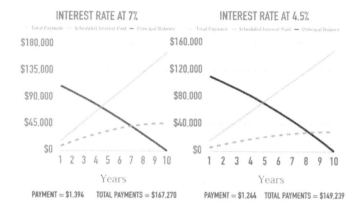

$120,000 IN DEBT OVER 10 YEARS
(WHEN INTEREST RATE DROPS FROM 7% TO 4.5%)

INTEREST RATE AT 7%

PAYMENT = \$1,394   TOTAL PAYMENTS = \$167,270

INTEREST RATE AT 4.5%

PAYMENT = \$1,244   TOTAL PAYMENTS = \$149,239

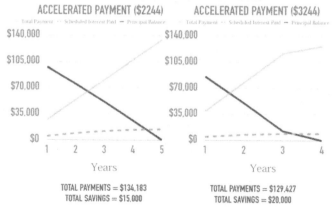

$120,000 IN DEBT OVER 10 YEARS
(PAYING AN EXTRA \$1000 AND \$2000 PER MONTH)

ACCELERATED PAYMENT (\$2244)

TOTAL PAYMENTS = \$134,183
TOTAL SAVINGS = \$15,000

ACCELERATED PAYMENT (\$3244)

TOTAL PAYMENTS = \$129,427
TOTAL SAVINGS = \$20,000

Access tools at:
http://student.byeloandebt.com/calculators/

So, how did I calculate these savings and other scenarios? Although I could have done it by hand, I relied heavily on a loan calculator (Shameless plug: go to https://student.byeloandebt.com/calculators/ for this loan tool and more). This calculator allowed me to easily input different options, such as accelerated payments, so that we could quickly understand the effects of adjusting our monthly payments up or down. Here are two examples of how adjusting our payments would affect our overall repayment cost and schedule:

- If we dedicated $1,000 more than our minimum payment per month on a ten-year loan, the length of our loan repayment period would HALVE from ten years to five years, for a total savings of $15,000 ($134,000 versus $149,000 in total payments)

- If we dedicated $2,000 more than our minimum payment per month, the length of our loan repayment term would be reduced to three years, with a total savings of $20,000 ($129,000 versus $149,000 in total payments).

We used this tool to determine how much we needed to pay off per month in order to reach our loan repayment goal. You can play with all of these scenarios based on your personal situation. Use the same website calculator tools we have used throughout the book.

Our new amortization (payoff) table with our

improved interest rates (pictured below) shows that we needed to pay $150 less per month than what we had originally expected to meet our five-year loan repayment goal (Page 19). This shows the power of reducing interest rates!

YEAR	BALANCE	YEARLY PAY.	INT. PAY.	PRINC. PAY.	END BALANCE
1	$130,000.00	$29,612.91	$5,850	$23,762	$106,237
2	$107,398.72	$29,612.91	$4,780	$24,832	$81,404
3	$83,213.09	$29,612.91	$3,663	$25,949	$55,455
4	$57,332.05	$29,612.91	$2,495	$27,117	$28,337
5	$29,636.74	$29,612.91	$1,275	$28,337	–

After seven years of school and over six figures of student loan debt, my wife and I had finally landed full-time jobs and simplified our student loans to have the best possible interest rates. Now, we knew that if we could just scrape together $2,423 a month with our combined incomes, we would eliminate all student loan debt within our five-year goal!

Our example is an extreme one in terms of our overall debt level, as well as our aggressive repayment goals. Depending on your financial situation, your goals, and a host of other factors, your situation could be very similar or very different than what I have outlined here. However, the principles are the same and the customizable tools outlined here will allow you to address your unique situation. By following the principles, you will be able to reduce your debt burden no matter your situation. Say BYE to Beat Your Extensive debt!

Now that you know how to reduce your student loan debt, you need to know how much: How much do you pay towards each loan and which loan should you pay off first? How much do you contribute to other financial investments or life decisions and how do you decide? The answers are simple compared to what you have done so far - and they are the subject of the next chapter.

Key Takeaways:

- When beginning to make loan payments or when your deferral period is nearing, setup minimum automatic payments with your loan to reduce interest rates

- Loan consolidation is your friend; use it to reduce interest rates and gain more favorable loan terms to decrease your payoff period and total debt payments

- Government loans provide more forgiving repayment terms while private loans allow for more flexible loan consolidations

- As a general rule, fixed interest loans have higher rates and should be used for longer time horizons, while variable have lower interest rates and should be used for shorter time horizons

- Use the payoff tool outlined in this chapter to determine how loan consolidation, reduced interest rates, and accelerated payments can help to decrease your payoff period and total payment

CHAPTER FOUR

TIME TO TAKE ACTION

The rubber has finally met the road and you can now put your plan in action! At this point, you may have one simple consolidated loan for a few thousand dollars, or you may have six figures of debt across five to ten lenders, all with varying interest rates. No matter your situation, you need to know the most efficient way to pay off these loans and reduce your overall costs in the long-term. Saying BYE to your loan debt should always be handled in coordination with balancing other financial decisions in life, such as contributing to your 401k, buying a house, or preparing to have children.

If you followed my advice back in Chapter 3 (Bargain Hunting), you should have already set up automatic payments on all of your loans. This means that you are paying the minimum payment for each loan across all of your debt. This will ensure that you do not miss any payments - which could adversely affect your credit. This money will be automatically withdrawn from your checking account every month.

Now it's time to adjust your budget to reflect these automated monthly payments. Simply add up all the minimum payments you make for one month. Next, take the sum that you just calculated and subtract it from the budget you created in Chapter 2 (Ballin' on a Budget Requires a Plan). Below is an example that is completely hypothetical. I've created it to represent the budget of a recent master's degree graduate with a full-time job.

MONTHLY INCOME	$4,167
OTHER (TUTORING, COACHING, ETC.)	$100
TOTAL MONTHLY INCOME	**$4,267**
401K CONTRIBUTION	$250
TAXES	$750
CAR LOAN	$200
CAR INSURANCE	$100
LIVING EXPENSES (RENT, UTILITIES, GAS, ETC.)	$1,500
OTHER (ENTERTAINMENT, TRAVEL, ETC.)	$300
TOTAL MONTHLY EXPENSES	**$3,100**
MINIMUM LOAN PAYMENT	$356
MONTHLY NET	**$811**

Access tools at:
http://student.byeloandebt.com/calculators/

The new 'True Monthly Net Income' represents the extra money the hypothetical graduate has after all normal expenses, including the sum of all minimum monthly payments on his or her student loans. In this example, the recent graduate has approximately $30,000 in student loans over a ten-year term. Again, your situation may dramatically differ from this, but the principles are the same. For simplicity's sake, let's say the $30,000 in student loan debt is spread across two different loans. One is a federally owned government loan for $10,000 at 6.8% interest and the other is a $20,000 loan from a private bank with an interest rate of 3.5%. Using the budget above, this recent graduate would have an additional $800 in net income after minimum loan payments are made and all other living expenses are paid. With this $800, the student has the following options:

- Blow it all at the bars on weekends or whichever form of entertainment he or she prefers

- Purchase a bunch of Shake Weights or steak knives from infomercials

- Save this money for a rainy day

- Contribute this money towards investments (i.e. 401k/IRA, house, stocks, etc.)

- Aggressively pay off his or her loans

What would you do?[7] Since you've made it this far

---

[7] It is always important to ensure you build a safety fund for life events and emergencies, such as car breakdowns, an unexpected hospital run, or any of life's other surprises. Sixty percent of all Americans cannot afford a

in the book, you are likely looking to implement the third, fourth or fifth option (Although, those late night infomercials are tempting!). It is also likely that you're weighing the benefits of each of those three choices against each other. After all, each additional dollar you invest is another dollar you are not contributing towards paying off your student loans. For that reason, it is helpful to find a balance of aggressively paying off your loans, and beginning or continuing to invest in your future and retirement. No matter what percent of your net income you spend on student loans, you will likely have this decision to make.

If you have one simple loan at this point, then you can ignore this next example (as you would simply contribute your extra funds each month to that single loan). However, in the hypothetical example we have created above, the recent graduate still has two student loans to choose between:

- $20,000 in loans at an interest rate of 6.5%

- $10,000 in loans at an interest rate of 3.5%

Which loan do you make extra payment towards? How much of your extra money do you contribute to

---

$500 unexpected expense. Don't become one of those people! Before you become too aggressive with paying your student loans down, you should always aim to have a minimum of two to three months of living expenses stashed away in the bank. In the example above, if the recent graduate has zero dollars in his or her bank account, it would be wise to save the $800 net income for several months BEFORE beginning to pay down his or her debt. This will prevent the recent graduate from getting into a situation in which he or she does not have funds for emergency expenses.

each loan? The answer is simple, but potentially counterintuitive for some of you. (Don't scoff finance majors; we didn't all go to school for that!). Many of you may think it makes sense to pay the loan with the lower remaining balance, as it will be paid off quicker.

If that is what you think, you are wrong - just as I was when I first started thinking about my payments. No matter how much debt you own for one loan, whether it is $100 or $100,000, the higher interest rate loan ALWAYS costs you more money. Let's take a loan of $100 as an example. At 6.5% you will pay $6.50 every year on that loan, while at 3.5% you will pay $3.50 on that same loan. A higher interest rate equates to a more expensive loan every time. For this reason, you should always contribute your accelerated payments towards the loan(s) with the highest interest rate(s) first. The only exception to this is if you simply need a moral victory. If you have five different loans, but one of them can be paid off with one month of net income, you may consider paying this off, even if it has a lower interest rate. Why is this the exception? For one, it would simplify your debt situation; secondly, it may provide a much-needed physiological boost towards eliminating your debt in the long run AND it may encourage you to stick with the principles outlined in this book. Just be aware that if you adopt this method, you are not paying your loans off in the most efficient and cost effective method possible.

Let's put you in the shoes of the example of the recent graduate above. Say you choose to spend your entire net income, $800 dollars, on student loans.

Which loan should you contribute the money to? By now, you probably know that it's wisest to put it towards the $20,000 in federally owned debt because of its 6.5% interest rate. This will result in the most efficient method to pay off your debt.

Of course, it is critical for you to continue to make the minimum payments on ALL loans in order to avoid missed payments or default, which will hurt your credit. Once the $20,000 of federally owned debt is completely paid off, then you may want to shift all of your extra net income towards the $10,000 in debt at the 3.5% interest rate. If you follow this formula, your results will be eye opening.

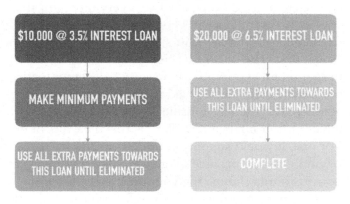

In this scenario of a total loan burden of $30,000 over ten years, if you were able to contribute an extra $800 to your loans each month, and you paid the highest interest loans first, your average interest rate would be approximately 5.5%. You would save over $7,000 dollars and enjoy an extra seven years of debt-free living! The more debt you have, the greater these savings will be in terms of money and time. In this example, had you paid your LOWER interest rate loans off first, you would end up spending an extra $500 for absolutely no reason other than you chose the wrong loan to pay off first! These savings will allow you to begin your debt-free adult life your way! You'll be able to take these extra savings and contribute them towards a down payment for a house or car, towards 401k/IRA investments, or towards a rewarding vacation to celebrate being debt-free.

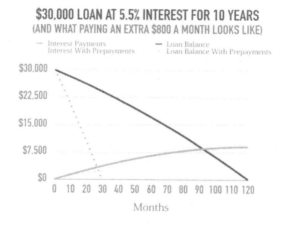

$30,000 LOAN AT 5.5% INTEREST FOR 10 YEARS
(AND WHAT PAYING AN EXTRA $800 A MONTH LOOKS LIKE)

— Interest Payments
  Interest With Prepayments

— Loan Balance
  Loan Balance With Prepayments

Months

In this jaw-dropping example, you are able to see how much money you can MAKE over the original loan time period - not just how much you can save. Let's say you are able to pay off your loans faster than the original term period of the loan. Clearly, you have developed a life skill – budgeting – and it would be silly to just drop this skill after your loans are paid off. After all, you now have a budgeting system in place and it would be easy to take the money that you once dedicated to student loan debt and now dedicate it towards investments.

SAVINGS WITH ACCELERATED PAYMENT PLAN

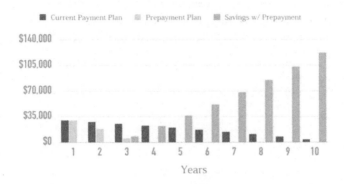

■ Current Payment Plan   ■ Prepayment Plan   ■ Savings w/ Prepayment

Years

For example, if you simply took your minimum monthly loan payments from the above example and contributed these towards an investment (rather than student loan debt, like you would have done previously) and this investment attained 5% growth (S&P 500's historical average is 9.8%), you would have over $120,000 invested! Over a ten-year period, rather than paying almost $40,000 in loan payments, you would pay about $31,000 in loan payments and have a sizeable nest egg of $120,000. This is all possible simply by making accelerated payments and picking the right loans to pay off first. This shows the true power of saying BYE to your debt by quickly and efficiently getting out of debt and getting your life on track without student loans!

To fully illustrate the lesson of this chapter, let's take a more complex scenario. This example may be more typical of a student with larger debt problems. In this example, let's assume the student borrower has the following debts:

- $20,000 in student loans at an interest rate of 6.5%
- $10,000 in student loans at an interest rate of 3.5%
- $4,000 in car loans at an interest rate of 5.5%
- $15,000 in credit card debt at an interest rate of 18.0%

Given this scenario, which debt would you pay off first? If you have learned the lessons within this chapter, you would prioritize the loans above in the following manner:

- $15,000 in credit card debt at an interest rate of 18.0%
- $20,000 in student loans at an interest rate of 6.5%
- $4,000 in car loans at an interest rate of 5.5%
- $10,000 in student loans at an interest rate of 3.5%

In order to pay off these debts in the quickest way, you would make minimum payments on all four loans. Then, you would take 100% of your extra net income and dedicate it towards your credit card debt until it is fully paid off. When it is paid off, you would apply your extra net income to the $20,000 student loan, followed by the $4,000 car loan, and lastly followed by the $10,000 student loan. Notice how this order has absolutely nothing to do with the overall amount of debt for each loan, but it is instead in descending order based solely on the interest rate of each loan.

One thing that you may have noticed in the example above is the incredibly high interest rate of 18.0% on credit card interest! I used this example specifically to discuss credit card debt, as millions of Americans have credit card debt situations very similar to this. I cannot stress enough how destructive this 'bad debt' can be for your financial situation. Not only is it probable that this debt is not serving a purpose other than discretionary spending, but the outrageous interest rates can easily cause your debt to spiral out of control. If you make minimum payments of $25 dollars a month on $15,000 of credit card interest at 18% interest, you will end up paying $30,000 and it will take you twenty years to pay off this debt! In reality, many credit card companies may or may not have terms that force higher payments; either way, this situation will still be detrimental to your financial freedom. At all costs, I highly recommend that you work to consolidate credit card debt, if it is at all possible, as outlined in Chapter 3. If you are unable to for some reason, all extra net income should be fully dedicated to ridding yourself of this cursed debt.

While the above credit card debt is not good, responsible credit card use has many positive benefits. My wife and I currently have about 5 credit cards between the two of us, which have the following benefits:

- 1-2% cash back on all purchases
- Extended warranties on large purchases
- Points that can be used towards flights
- Travel insurance and various other perks
- Established credit card history

None of our credit cards have annual fees and we automatically pay our complete balance the following month before interest accumulates. This effectively gives us a one-month interest free loan and cash back that we use to pay off all of our purchases, along with the other benefits listed above.

Furthermore, this can positively help your credit score. My father gave me a credit card when I was fifteen years old. I was allowed to use the card on gas payments (once I was of driving age) and for emergency situations. I continued the responsible use of this credit card through college and into my early adult life. By paying off the credit card balance each month in full, and never missing a payment on my credit card or any other bills, I had a credit score of 760 when I turned twenty-five years old. This credit score put me in the top 10% of all Americans. Additionally, this score is what allowed me to get very favorable loan consolidations for my wife, an extremely favorable loan home mortgage rate of 3.675%, and 0.5% interest on my sixty-month car loan. Once you are able to eliminate credit card debt, I highly recommend the use of credit cards to build credit – but only if you can have the discipline to use the card(s) responsibly.

If you have absorbed the last four chapters, you

should have all of the tools and information necessary to understand and execute on a debt freedom plan. Once you make it to this step in the process, the rest of your student loan repayment should be on cruise control until you can start the next chapter of your life – one without the burden of student loan debt! You are one step closer to saying BYE to Beat Your Extensive debt!

Key Takeaways:

- Calculate your new monthly net income by taking into account the minimum payments required for every loan; this will determine the extra money you have to pay down your loans quicker

- Extra monthly income should always be paid towards the highest interest rate loans first in order to most efficiently pay off the debt; continue to make minimum payments on all other loans to avoid late payments or default

- Use the payoff tool outlined in this chapter to determine how extra monthly net income can be used to lower your total payments and payoff period

- Accelerated payments can allow you to start focusing on growing your retirement nest egg and getting on with your financial life without student loan debt

5 STEPS TO GET RID OF YOUR STUDENT LOANS

STEP 01 — ASSESS YOUR SITUATION
STEP 02 — CREATE A BUDGET
STEP 03 — SET A GOAL
STEP 04 — RESTRUCTURE & REFINANCE
STEP 05 — EXECUTE, MANAGE & ADJUST

CHAPTER FIVE

CRUISE CONTROL TO A DEBT-FREE LIFE

You are now at the last step! At this point, all that you must do is monitor your debt situation, make minor adjustments and cruise to a debt-free life. This section will cover one of the easiest portions of this process - but it may prove to be one of the most critical. This part requires that you react to changing market conditions, monitor your current financial situation and continually execute your debt goal. I recommend you look into your financial life approximately every three months. This will give you enough time to adapt to changing situations, but not too frequently to become burdened or stressed out from things that are beyond your control.

The best way to start this step is to pull up your student debt plan, monthly budget and amortization table from Chapter 2 (Ballin' on a Budget Requires a Plan). From this, you can create some sort of tracker using the online calculator tools linked to this book. Every three months, you should update your monthly income and net income in a file such as the example below. As the months and years go by, you may see your monthly income go up with promotions or job changes, and you will likely see fluctuations in expenses. These fluctuations are common, and occur as the results of changing living situations, moving to new cities, starting or finishing car payments, etc. It is important to constantly monitor your True Monthly Net Income so that you can dedicate any surpluses towards paying off your loans. This should take no more than fifteen minutes every three months. This is the first step in monitoring your debt situation.

MONTHLY INCOME	$4,167
OTHER (TUTORING, COACHING, ETC.)	$100
TOTAL MONTHLY INCOME	**$4,267**
401K CONTRIBUTION	$250
TAXES	$750
CAR LOAN	$200
CAR INSURANCE	$100
BASIC LIVING EXPENSES (RENT, UTILITIES, GAS, ETC.)	$1,500
OTHER (ENTERTAINMENT, TRAVEL, ETC.)	$300
TOTAL MONTHLY EXPENSES	**$3,100**
MONTHLY NET	**$1,167**
MINIMUM LOAN PAYMENT	$356
TRUE MONTHLY NET	**$811**

Access tools at:
http://student.byeloandebt.com/calculators/

The second part of this exercise is monitoring each one of your loans and adjusting the total amount of debt left on each, including any interest. You must also monitor the terms so that you are aware of any changes. Every three months, my wife and I adjusted the total debt for each loan, the total debt of all loans added together, interest rates, and any other terms that changed over the prior months. This looked like the following:

LOAN SOURCE	TOTAL DEBT	IR (%)	FIX. OR VAR.	TERMS
SOFI	$55,000	5.38	FIX	5 YEAR TERM
GREAT LAKES	$23,000	3.58	FIX	15 YEARS LEFT ON TERM
WELLS FARGO	$33,929	3.75	VAR	6 MONTHS AFTER GRADUATION
TOTAL	$111,929	4.51		

This is extremely important for of the following reasons:

1. If you are following your plan correctly, one loan should be decreasing more rapidly compared to the others. In the example above, we wanted to make sure the SOFI loan (which had the highest interest rate) was decreasing the fastest when compared to the other loans. This is important to show that your extra monthly income is being 100% dedicated to your highest interest loan.

2. In doing this exercise every three months, you will likely see a significant reduction in at least one of your loans. This will provide you a psychological boost and keep you committed to your plan.

3. By completing this exercise, you are also able to ensure that none of your terms have

changed in ways that may affect payments or anything else. This is especially important if you own variable interest loans, as shifting market conditions will affect your interest rate. In the personal example of my wife and I, I paid special attention to the Wells Fargo loan every few months to monitor fluctuations in the variable interest rate. If it ever rose above 5.38%, I had an action plan in place. First, I would reprioritize this loan over the SOFI loan; this way, my wife and I would be able to pay off the loan with the highest interest rate (now, the Wells Fargo loan) with our extra monthly incomes. Next, I would shop for more favorable terms in a potentially new loan.

Mortgage rates

30-year fixed — 15-year fixed — 1-year ARM

Source: Bankrate.com

While digging into the updated details on each of your loans, you may want to look into the general interest rate situation within the market. You can very easily Google 'National Interest Rates' to see what the approximate interest rates are in the market. If your original student loans or your consolidated loans were executed in the late 1990's to late 2000's, it is likely that you have received interest rates that are much higher than they are currently. If you followed the rules of consolidating loans in Chapter 3 (Bargain Hunting), then it is possible that you were successful in lowering your interest rates to get the best terms available. However, if it has been many years, or if there have been dramatic changes in interest rates as a result of a financial event, there is a possibility that you will be able to refinance or negotiate with current lenders for a lower interest rate.

In my personal situation, I was never able to find more favorable terms throughout the life of each loan, so we had no need to make adjustments to our terms or with our lenders. This may or may not be true as your unique situation unfolds.

The third and final portion of this phase is monitoring your overall progress. At the end of Chapter 2 (Ballin' on a Budget Requires a Plan), I showed you an amortization tool. This tool demonstrated the annual and monthly payments required for you to be able to completely pay off your loans within the time period that you selected as a goal. For my situation, I selected a five-year goal, so the amortization tool looked like this:

YEAR	BALANCE	MON. PAY.	INT. PAY.	PRINC. PAY.	END BALANCE
1	$130,000.00	$2,483	$7,150	$23,292	$106,707
2	$106,707.06	$2,483	$5,868	$24,574	$82,133
3	$82,133.02	$2,483	$4,517	$25,925	$56,207
4	$56,207.39	$2,483	$3,091	$27,351	$28,855
5	$28,855.86	$2,483	$1,587	$28,855	-

In order to be successful at paying off your loans by the desired date you set, you will have to make sure that your monthly net income is more than the monthly payment required in your personal amortization table.

- After doing this analysis four times a year, you will determine one of three scenarios:
- You are meeting your monthly goals and your monthly net income is in line with your monthly payment goal;
- Your monthly net income is greater than your monthly payment goal; or
- Your monthly net income is less than your monthly payment goal.

In the first situation, your plan is being executed perfectly to schedule; so, congratulations! In the second scenario, you deserve a gold star for being ahead of plan. You can use your extra monthly income to even more aggressively pay off your loans.

Now, let's talk about the third scenario. If at any point in the process you see yourself in this scenario, it is time to reassess your monthly net income and your debt goals. This scenario leaves you with three different options:

- Increase your monthly income through an extra job or overtime.
- Decrease your monthly expenses to increase your net income.
- Change your debt goals so that you have a longer time horizon to become debt-free.

While none of these situations are ideal, life happens. Not everyone will be able to stick completely to his or her original plan. If you refuse to extend your repayment term and are insistent on sticking to your goals, then it is time to roll up your sleeves and search for additional income or methods to reduce your expenses. Consider doing side jobs, such as tutoring, landscaping, or becoming a part time Uber driver. Additionally, reduce costs by cutting ties with your cable TV, adding a roommate to share monthly costs, eating in to avoid bar and restaurant tabs, carpooling to and from work with friends and colleagues, or doing anything else that will help you to lower your monthly bills.

By performing these three simple steps for about thirty minutes, four times a year, you will be able to adequately monitor, track and adjust all of your debt to ensure you are meeting your goals and are most effectively eliminating your debt! The remaining chapters of this book include methods to employ when you are struggling to make minimum payments, things to do with your money when you are debt-free, and ways to avoid getting in large amounts of debt in the first place. The first five chapters have given you a blueprint on how to eliminate your debt. If you have followed my advice so far, but you are still struggling to pay off your loans, the next chapter is for you.

Key Takeaways:

- Make sure to monitor your loan situation every three months to ensure your plan is being enacted appropriately and that no action is need to further adjust loan payment priorities or consolidation terms

- Use the amortization tool to ensure your payments are on track to meet your goals

- If you have departed from your goals, look for methods to increase your monthly net income by adding additional income or cutting unnecessary expenses

5 STEPS TO GET RID OF YOUR STUDENT LOANS

STEP 01 ASSESS YOUR SITUATION

STEP 02 CREATE A BUDGET

STEP 03 SET A GOAL

STEP 04 RESTRUCTURE & REFINANCE

STEP 05 EXECUTE, MANAGE & ADJUST

CHAPTER SIX

WHEN YOU HIT A WALL

In an ideal world, you will have read the first five chapters of this book, instituted your personal plan, and put your loans on cruise control. However, we all know that life is rarely perfect. If you are struggling to make your payments or you have a massive amount of debt with no feasible means to pay it off, this chapter will cover a number of tactics that can be employed to delay, forgive or reduce your debt when you do not have the financial means to eliminate it yourself. Keep in mind that all of these tactics will likely extend or increase your loans, contrary to the principles outlined so far in this book (unless you are one of the few that qualify for forgiveness or discharge). More often than not, these tactics should only be used as a last resort.

Below is a comprehensive list taken from the government student loan webpage that outlines all of the options for student loan forgiveness, cancellation or discharge. If you find yourself falling into a situation where you cannot make your payments, **DO NOT CONSOLIDATE** your federal student loans into a private loan. The programs below only apply to eligible federal student loans, **NOT** private loans. This is one of the most important reasons not to consolidate or change your federal student loan terms if you are struggling to meet the minimum monthly payments.

TYPE OF FORGIVENESS, CANCELLATION OR DISCHARGE	DIRECT LOANS	FEDERAL FAMILY EDUCATION LOAN (FFEL)	PERKINS LOANS
CLOSED SCHOOL DISCHARGE	X	X	X
TOTAL AND PERMANENT DISABILITY DISCHARGE	X	X	X
DEATH DISCHARGE	X	X	X
DISCHARGE IN BANKRUPTCY (RARE)	X	X	X
FALSE CERTIFICATION OF STUDENT ELIGIBILITY OR UNAUTHORIZED PAYMENT DISCHARGE	X	X	
UNPAID REFUND DISCHARGE	X	X	
TEACHER LOAN FORGIVENESS	X	X	
PUBLIC SERVICE LOAN FORGIVENESS	X		
PERKINS LOAN CANCELLATION AND DISCHARGE			X
BORROWER DEFENSE DISCHARGE	X	X	

Chart[8]

The first few scenarios are categorized as discharges. Discharges usually occur in rare situations concerning life-altering or extenuating circumstances outside of the borrower's control. In these scenarios, a student loan can be discharged; this means that the student borrower would be completely relieved of student loan payment obligations. Here are the scenarios that can lead to loan discharges for you:

- Your school closes and you are unable to complete your program/degree OR your school closes within 120 days of you withdrawing from a program.
- You have become totally or permanently disabled.
- You become deceased – which is obviously not the case if you are reading this book (unless you've been cryogenically frozen!). However, this is very important information for the spouse of a deceased student borrower, who would normally incur his or her deceased partner's debt.
- You become bankrupt and can prove to the bankruptcy court that "repaying your student loans would cause undue hardship." This in itself is very difficult to do; it is expensive, crushing to your long-term future, and it is extremely rare. You cannot simply pull a Michael Scott from The Office and say, "I declare bankruptcy." Instead, you would need to prove the following: 1) If you are forced to repay the loan, you would not be able to maintain a minimal standard of living; 2) There is evidence that this hardship will continue for a significant portion of the loan

repayment period; 3) You made good-faith efforts to repay the loan before filing bankruptcy. (Usually this means you have been in repayment for a minimum of five years.)

- Your loan was falsely certified because of one of the following: 1) Your school signed an application/promissory note without your permission; 2) You were a victim of identity theft; 3) You incorrectly certified that you were eligible to benefit from a loan; 4) You are disqualified from participating in the workforce in the area your degree was attained for reasons such as mental condition, criminal record, etc.
- You withdrew from school, but your school failed to pay a refund to the US Department of Education for your loan amount.
- Your school committed fraud under local state laws.

If any of the above circumstances apply to your situation, you may be eligible for partial or complete discharge of your student loans. However, please keep this in mind: In each of the scenarios above, there are various rules and qualifications that limit eligibility and determine the number of loans that will be affected (discharged). To find out more, visit the following website to read about your personal eligibility and to discover the process for reporting these types of circumstances: https://studentaid.ed.gov/sa/repay-loans/forgiveness-cancellation. If you do apply for any of these scenarios, make sure to contact your loan servicer immediately to determine the exact process for application.

While you may become eligible for one of these scenarios during your student loan repayment period, eligibility is not something to long for. Becoming eligible for one of the categories above is *extremely* rare and eligibility is almost always the result of unfathomable personal and financial hardship. Although loan discharges may seem like a positive outcome, they are the result of circumstances far worse than repaying student loan debt.

In less extreme examples, where financial hardships and situations cause temporary interruptions in student loan repayments, you may want to consider forbearance or deferment options. These will help you through brief setbacks in your life.

Deferment is a period in which your principle and the interest associated with your federal loans are temporarily delayed for a period of up to three years. During this time period, the federal government pays your principle and interest on Federal Perkins loans, Direct Subsidized loans, and subsidized federal Stafford loans. If you have a loan that is unsubsidized, the government pays the principle and you are still responsible for the interest. You can apply for deferment in any of the following scenarios:

- While you are enrolled at least half-time at an eligible college or career school, and if you received a Direct PLUS Loan or FFEL PLUS Loan as a graduate or professional student, for an additional six months after you cease to be enrolled at least half-time (In-School Deferment Request)

- If you are a parent who received a Direct PLUS Loan or a FFEL PLUS Loan, while the student for whom you obtained the loan is enrolled at least half-time at an eligible college or career school, and for an additional six months after the student ceases to be enrolled at least half-time (Parent PLUS Borrower Deferment Request)

- While you are enrolled in an approved graduate fellowship program (Graduate Fellowship Deferment Request);
- While you are enrolled in an approved rehabilitation training program for the disabled (Rehabilitation Training Program Deferment Request)

- While you are unemployed or unable to find full-time employment, for up to three years (Unemployment Deferment Request)

- While you are experiencing economic hardship or serving in the Peace Corps, for up to three years (Economic Hardship Deferment Request)

- While you are on active duty military service in connection with a war, military operation, or national emergency (Military Service and Post-Active Duty Student Deferment Request)

- If you were on active duty military service in connection with a war, military operation, or national emergency, for the 13 month period following the conclusion of that service, or until you return to college or career school on at least a half-time basis, whichever is earlier (Military Service and Post-Active Duty Student Deferment Request).[9]

After you determine that you qualify for one of the above, contact your loan servicer and begin the application process.

If you are unable to qualify for deferment, a less attractive but helpful option is forbearance. With the option of forbearance, you are allowed to delay making payments to your loan servicer for a period of up to one year. While you are free from making payments, interest will still accrue on all loans during this time period.

There are two types of forbearance options: mandatory and discretionary. Under discretionary forbearance, your lender can use its discretion to grant forbearance due to financial hardship or illness; this means that the lender assesses your situation and uses its judgment to determine what terms you deserve. In contrast, mandatory forbearance requires your lender to grant forbearance. Mandatory forbearance is only applicable if you meet one of the following criteria:

- You are in a medical or dental internship/residency program and meet certain requirements.
- Your monthly student loan payments are greater than 20% of your monthly income.

---

9   https://studentaid.ed.gov/sa/repay-loans/forgiveness-cancellation/charts

- You received a national service award in a national service position.
- You are performing a teaching service that would apply for loan forgiveness (more on this later).
- You qualify for partial repayment of your loans (more on this later).
- You are not eligible for military deferment, but you have been activated as part of the National Guard.

If you are eligible for either deferment or forbearance, contact your loan servicer to provide necessary documentation to begin the application process.

As a reminder, while all of these options will provide temporary relief, they each carry long-term implications; ultimately these options will extend the length of your overall payment schedule and increase the amount you must repay. Both deferment and forbearance should be used as last resorts; and unfortunately, these will dramatically impair your ability to meet your loan repayment goals.

So what happens if you don't apply for any of the options listed above, or if you're simply not eligible for them? Do not panic. There are still additional options if you are struggling to make your minimum monthly payments. Relief can sometimes come in the form of altering your repayment terms. Under a standard repayment plan, you agree to pay off your loans with a fixed payment schedule over a ten-year period. In some cases, these payment terms can be modified based on your financial situation. If you're failing to meet you minimum monthly payments, the following options may be available through your loan servicer:

Graduated Repayment Plan – This plan is set up for a ten-year repayment period, like most standard loans; however, earlier years in the loan repayment period have smaller payments and these become bigger over time. This effectively allows more interest to accrue in the first few years, which ultimately means that you'll pay more towards your loan over its lifetime. The benefit, though, is that you have greater relief in the early years of repayment. This is a good option for those who are currently struggling and expect to have increases in income over time.

Extended Repayment Plan – If you have over $30,000 in student loans, you can extend your payments to up to twenty-five years. This means that you will have considerably smaller payments, but pay significantly more in loans over the overall term. As outlined in previous chapters, this is the result of increasing the amount of interest accrued over the length of the loan, which causes you to pay significantly more over the term.

Pay As You Earn (PAYE) or Revised Pay As You Earn (REPAYE) plan – Under these plans, your loan payment will be set at no more than 10% of your discretionary income. If you continue to make these payments for a twenty or twenty-five year period, depending on your qualifications, the remaining loan balance will be completely forgiven. Despite the loan being forgiven, you will likely end up paying significantly more towards your loan than in a traditional payment plan. This plan is usually wise for someone looking to participate in a Public Service Loan Forgiveness program (PSLF). We will discuss more on this later.

Income Based Repayment Plan (IBR), Income Contingent Repayment Plan (ICR), or Income Sensitive Repayment Plan (ISR) – Each of these repayment options is similar to the PAYE and REPAYE plans; however, these plans vary in the types of loans that apply, the percentage of discretionary income that you repay, and the length of repayment period. Each of these, like PAYE and REPAYE, forgive the remaining balance on a loan after a twenty-year period or more, and all three may be good options for someone seeking a Public Service Loan Forgiveness program (PSLF). Similarly, despite loan forgiveness, you will end up paying more over the total term of this loan than if you were to execute a traditional repayment plan.

Your final (and possibly best) option - if you are struggling to make payments or if you have a massive amount of debt relative to your income - is to seek loan forgiveness through a variety of programs. These options not only allow you to have your loans forgiven, but they also provide you with the opportunity to perform civic duties. This is why the government incentivizes students to enroll in these programs. You can apply for a Public Service Loan Forgiveness program (PSLF) if you work for one of the following:

- A government organization at any level (tribal, local, state, federal)
- A not-for-profit organization that is tax exempt

under 501(c)(3)
- Other not-for-profit organizations such as AmeriCorps, Peace Corps, Teach for America, etc.

If you are a full-time employee (30+ hours per week) in any of the programs listed above and you've made 120 qualifying loan payments (ten years of loan payments) under one of the qualified repayment options outlined above, the remainder of your loan can be forgiven. If this situation applies to you, the PAYE, REPAYE, IBR, ICR, or ISR repayment plans will dramatically lower your monthly payment for the ten-year period you are required to pay before forgiveness. In this situation, as long as you will take at least ten years to repay your loan and you are working for a qualified PSLF employer, an income based repayment plan is a no-brainer. However, it is still important to realize that if you have the ability to pay your loans over a quicker time horizon, say three years, your overall loan repayment may still be lower than receiving loan forgiveness after ten years of lower monthly payments. The online tools outlined in this book can help to guide you through these scenarios so that you can make the best choice possible.

Another program that the federal government offers is the Teacher Loan Forgiveness Program (TLFP). Under this program, if you serve as an educator for five complete, consecutive years in low income and other qualified areas, you may be eligible to receive $17,500 in loan forgiveness of Direct or Stafford subsidized and unsubsidized loans.

Finally, if you have received a Perkins loan (a financial need-based lower interest loan), you may also have the opportunity for complete loan cancellation if you take part in any of the following professions, programs or organizations:

- Volunteer in Peace Corps or ACTION program
- Teacher
- Member of the U.S. armed forces
- Nurse or medical technician
- Law enforcement or corrections officer
- Head Start worker
- Child or family services worker
- Provider of early intervention services

So there you have it. If you are in a sticky situation, there are a plethora of opportunities to help delay, forgive, discharge or cancel your loans completely. For the vast majority of student loan borrowers, most of these options may not apply immediately; however, they can be employed through simple life and career choices. If you have a massive amount of debt and an affinity for public service, the various loan forgiveness programs our government offers provide a win-win situation.

Please note, current government officials have hinted that these programs may end in the near future; so, it is always wise to assume programs like this will not exist forever. If the need exists, use this program if you can, while you can.

Hopefully, this chapter taught you how to say **BYE** and **B**eat **Y**our **E**xtensive debt through alternative methods. Now, in Chapter 7, you will have the opportunity to learn about managing your financial life when you are debt-free.

Key Takeaways:

- If you fall behind in your repayment goals or are in a bad situation, there are a number of tactics you can employ to delay, forgive, discharge, or cancel your student loans.

- The federal government provides many flexible repayment options to extend the length of payments. These will almost always increase the total amount of your payments, but may provide temporary relief so that you can maintain making your minimum monthly payments.

- The federal government also provides many forgiveness programs tied to social work or personally challenging situations.

CHAPTER SEVEN

LIFE AFTER DEBT

Congratulations! You have all the tools to successfully create a student debt repayment plan; and hopefully, this is the last chapter of your student loan debt and the first chapter of your financial freedom. The content of this chapter can be, and has been, the subject matter of full-length books. While I have condensed many of the following principles to their most basic forms, these concepts should be used as guides as you get nearer to enjoying your debt-free life. It is critical for every student loan holder to understand what to do with his or her money as his or her debt lessens. Why? Many students will most likely be years behind in saving for retirement as a result of their massive college loans. If this is true of your situation, it is imperative for you to do one of the following:

1. Contribute to your retirement if you can also pay off your debt to meet the goals outlined in this book; or

2. Aggressively and proactively contribute to your retirement after you've paid off your student loan debt in order to meet your retirement goals.

Now, I know what you're thinking: When did we start talking about retirement goals?! But similarly to how the first step in this book is to create a goal around becoming debt-free, the first step in your debt-free life is creating a goal around retirement savings. Luckily, planning for retirement involves the same steps as escaping debt. You'll begin by creating a goal, building a budget, and then using those two items to determine how much you should contribute to your retirement investments.

Every student should begin thinking about retirement now. I know, I know, it sounds crazy, since you will not be retiring for another thirty or forty years, or more. But what you do in your twenties and thirties will have a disproportionate effect on how much money you have in retirement and at what age you can adequately retire.

To demonstrate this, let's say you are twenty-five and you plan to retire at age sixty-five; you have forty more years until retirement. Let's also say you contribute just over $300 a month for forty years to retirement. Over the years, you will hypothetically make about 8% on these investments, which is just below the average rate of return on stocks throughout the market's history. After forty years, you will have about $1,000,000! By contributing less than the amount that most people pay for a car loan, a little more than most pay for utilities, or less than most pay for groceries and entertainment, you could have $1,000,000 by the time you retire.

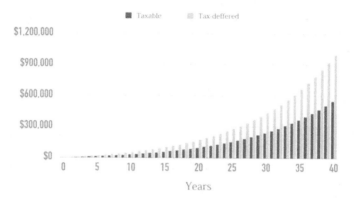

CONTRIBUTING $300 PER MONTH FROM AGE 25 - 65

However, now let's imagine that you are sixty-five. You are ready to live a great retirement, free from work. You are healthy and it is likely you will live until you are ninety-five - so, another thirty years. If you have ONLY saved $1,000,000, you will only have $33,000 dollars per year for all expenses including basic living and medical expenditures. One million dollars might sound like a ton of money today, but this will probably be insufficient for a lot of retirees, especially if they have a spouse, children and grandchildren, and/or want to travel the world and enjoy retirement.

Let's now go back to assuming you are twenty-five and let's pretend you do not contribute any money to your retirement savings until you are thirty-five because of overwhelming student loans. With all other variables held constant (8% interest, $300 a month), you would have less than $500,000. By contributing for ten fewer years than the person that begins at twenty-five, you would be missing out on half of the retirement nest egg. If you lived until you were ninety-five, you would only have approximately $16,000 to spend a year.

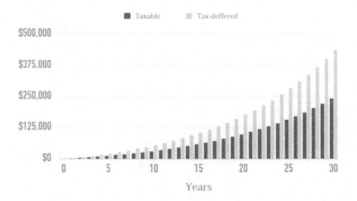

CONTRIBUTING $300 PER MONTH FROM AGE 35 – 65

There are very few retirees that spend this little each year of their lives. Compound interest, while it is your enemy in student loans, is your best friend in saving for retirement. The more years you save and the higher the interest rate on your investments, the more money you will have in the end!

The point of this example is two-fold. First, escaping debt as quickly as possible not only saves you money on the loans, but it also allows you to earn money for retirement (by investing your income instead of spending it paying off loans). Second, if you do not escape debt, you will not be able to save for retirement and you will end up working your entire life. If you have recently paid off all of your debts, or if you are able to contribute before you finish paying off your loans, you should begin contributing now! For my wife and I, we decided to use the same amount of money we used to pay in monthly student loans to invest in our retirement (once our student loans were paid off). This was an easy way to maintain the discipline we had grown accustomed to and continue to live under the same budget. Many will want to adjust this based on their needs after getting out of student loan debt, though.

Hopefully, if I have convinced you that this is important, you are now asking, "Ok, how do I do it?!"

There are dozens of different investment vehicles that allow you to invest money towards your retirement. Like I mentioned earlier, this one chapter could be a whole book. To maintain brevity, I will focus on some of the more important ones:

401k

A 401k is an investment vehicle that is usually set

up through your employer. (There are equivalents in special types of professions, like a 403b for teachers.) Each person (as of 2017), can contribute up to $18,000 pre-tax dollars per year to a 401k account, regardless of your income. Usually this payment comes directly out of your paycheck, pre-tax. This money is deducted from your earnings for the year. This means you pay fewer income taxes when you contribute to this retirement account. For example, if your adjusted gross income (AGI) is $50,000 one year, and you contribute $5,000 to your 401k, you only pay taxes on $45,000 of your income. Additionally, the money in this account grows tax-free. This money cannot be withdrawn, unless there is a qualified emergency or you feel like paying a hefty penalty tax, until you reach the age of fifty-nine and a half. At that point, you will be taxed at the future income tax rate for all distributions that you withdraw. This is especially advantageous if your taxes are expected to be similar or lower in retirement years compared to now.

Perhaps the most important feature of a 401k is the matching contributions that most employers provide. When you contribute to a company-sponsored 401k program, many companies offer to match a percentage of the money you contribute each month. For example, a company may match half of every contribution you make, up to 6% of your income. So, if you make $50,000 dollars and contribute 6% of your income, or $3,000, your employer will put $1,500 into that same retirement account. This is free money and should always be taken advantage of if possible! Although the employer does not match anything over

6%, any additional money that you contribute to the account (up to $18,000) still goes towards your retirement savings and lowers your tax burden. The only real downside of a 401k is that you are at the mercy of the plan to choose which investment options you have. Most employers limit this to a handful of investments that may not be perfect for your specific situation.

Traditional IRA

A traditional IRA works somewhat similarly to a 401k. In both instances, you can make pre-tax contributions to a retirement account. However, with an IRA, you can only contribute up to $5,500 a year (as of 2017). These contributions are tax deductible, assuming you make less than $61,000 dollars in AGI a year (for an individual, it is a different threshold for spouses); this means that if you make $50,000 and contribute $5,500, you only pay taxes on an income of $44,500. And the contributions are partially deductible if you make between $61,000 and $71,000.

One major difference between a 401k and an IRA is that an IRA is not setup through your employer; instead, you contribute as an individual to an IRA account through a banking institution, such as Schwab, Fidelity, or a number of other large institutions. This has one huge advantage: You are presented with a wide array of investment options that you individually select from. It is likely that you can choose from thousands of options, such as stocks, bonds, mutual funds, index funds and more.

A Traditional IRA, like a 401k, is also a good option for someone that expects his or her taxes to be similar or lower in the future. The money in your Traditional IRA grows tax-free. You can begin making taxed withdrawals once you reach the age of fifty-nine and a half.

Roth IRA

A Roth IRA is very similar to a Traditional IRA. The biggest difference here is that you make your contributions after you've paid tax on the income. This is a great option for young people that expect their income and tax bracket to increase into their retirement years. However, you do not receive the benefit of deducting these contributions from your current-year taxes. Instead these contributions will grow tax-free and can be withdrawn completely tax-free once you are age fifty-nine and a half. This option is fully available to anyone making less than $117,000 in AGI a year (for an individual); and it is only partially available to those making between $117,000 and $132,000 (as of 2017). You cannot contribute over $5,500 between a Roth and Traditional IRA, but you can contribute to both types of accounts as long as the total does not go above this number. In recent years, there has also been the advent of the Roth 401k. This is much less common as most employers do not offer it; but depending on your financial situation, it may be appropriate.

Health Savings Account (HSA)

If you have a high deductible health insurance plan,

you may be eligible to contribute to a health savings account. Under these plans, money that is contributed is tax-deductible, grows tax-free, and is withdrawn tax-free as long as it is spent on qualified healthcare expenses. As of 2017, the maximum individual contribution is $3,350 and the maximum family contribution is $6,750. This is a great option to cover all future medical expenses for you and your family.

Above are just a few of the investment and retirement vehicles at your disposal. I will cover one more very important education investment vehicle in the last chapter.

So, which retirement vehicle do you contribute to? The answer is highly dependent on your financial situation, but as a general rule, most experts would recommend you contribute in the following order of importance:

1. Contribute up to the percentage of your employer's matching contributions in your 401k. So if they match up to 6%, contribute 6%. This is free money you do not want to leave on the table!

2. If you still have money to contribute to retirement, contribute up to $5,500 dollars to a qualified Traditional or Roth IRA. For those who are young and expect to make significantly more by the time they retire, a Roth IRA is generally the best choice. For those that expect to make less and be in the same or lower tax bracket in retirement, a Traditional IRA may be best.

3. If you still have money to contribute to retirement, contribute the rest of the money required to get to the maximum allowable 401k contribution. If 6% of your income is $5,000, contribute an extra $13,000 annually to achieve the maximum contribution of $18,000 per year.

4. If you still have left over money, congratulations! You are one of few who have mastered the skill of saving! In this situation, you can start looking into non-retirement and tax beneficial vehicles such as HSAs, individual stocks, bonds, mutual funds, index funds, real estate investments, and the wider array of investment opportunities that exist.

My final recommendation (once you begin thinking about life after debt) is to gain a thorough understanding of your credit score and how to improve it. As I mentioned earlier in this book, I am a big fan of using credit cards to your advantage - as long as you can be responsible. For over thirteen years, I have been paying every expense possible on my credit cards and automatically withdrawing the balance from my bank account the following month. This allows me to avoid interest, build and improve my credit, and gain points and rewards. Additionally, it extends warranties on many large purchases and allows more favorable terms for purchases like a car or a house.

Credit cards are just one way to help improve your credit score, so you should examine all aspects of your credit to improve it. While many aspects of your credit score are quite silly, they will have a drastic effect on large purchases in the future such as a new car, a house, a wedding ceremony or any other purchase that accompanies a life event. The higher your score, the more beneficial your terms will be!

Key Takeaways:

- **Whether in loads of student debt or debt-free, it is never too early to begin investing.**

- **Retirement savings are heavily (and positively) influenced by compound interest rates - the very thing that is your enemy in student loans debt. Higher interest rates over longer periods of time will equate to a bigger nest egg in retirement.**

- **The sooner you can eliminate student debt and begin investing for retirement through the methods outlined in this chapter, the earlier you can retire stress-free!**

- **Make sure to improve your credit score for more favorable terms on future financing and purchasing events.**

CHAPTER EIGHT

HINDSIGHT IS 20/20

Hindsight is always 20/20. If we had known everything at age eighteen that we know now, many of us would probably have made different decisions back then. Sure, at the time, borrowing money to go to the school of our dreams seemed like a no-brainer – and many of us would still make that same decision today. However, perhaps we would have gone about it a different, smarter way. I have no doubt that some of us would have put a little more energy and legwork into applying for scholarships, rather than simply taking the way that seemed easiest at the time (borrowing money from the banks). Perhaps we would have considered going to community college for the first two years, and then transferring to a more expensive university. Maybe we would have gotten a job or a second job while we were studying – not for extra money at the bar, but instead to begin paying off our loans immediately. We may have even gone as far as choosing a different major - one that led to higher paying jobs to combat the amount of debt we were taking on.

For those of us who have already finished our schooling and therefore cemented our present financial situation, we cannot erase our history. There is only one way out, and that's through eliminating student loan burdens by following the advice laid out in previous chapters.

For those who have yet to go to college, for parents of kids in private K-12 schools and colleges, and for future parents, this final chapter will discuss all of the options at your disposal to reduce the amount of debt you agree to take on. It is broken out by the different stages in preparing to and beginning to pay for school tuition.

Saving for the Future

For parents and future parents, the first step in preparing to pay for your child's education is to start saving! While not all parents will help pay for their kids' educations, there are many tax-favorable savings options at your disposal if you want to help out with the burden of modern college tuition. (Students, just because your parents are financially assisting you doesn't mean you do not have a responsibility to learn about these plans and employ many of the other options for reducing tuition burdens that we will discuss later.) A brief overview of each of the best saving options is below:

529 College Plans – Most states have 529 plans and you can choose from an array of state options regardless of where you currently live. Similar to 401k accounts, 529 savings plans allow you to make pre-tax contributions and invest in a variety of options to grow your contributions tax-free. The money can then be withdrawn without taxes, as long as it is spent on qualified education expenses like tuition, books and supplies. The plans can vary significantly by type, so it is wise to do research before selecting a plan; you should choose the plan that best fits your financial life and goals. There is one drawback of 529 plans: If you do not end up having educational expenses, a penalty tax is incurred when funds are withdrawn. Make sure you consult a tax expert when the time comes for withdrawals. This will allow you to capitalize on tax credits like the American Opportunity Credit and still use 529 funds.

Prepaid Tuition Plans – If you are confident your child will be attending an in-state school, some states have prepaid tuition plans that allow you to buy tuition credits in advance of your child's attendance. With tuition rates continually rising, this allows parents to lock in lower tuition costs for future attendance. The money is reimbursed if the student chooses an out-of-state school.

Roth IRA – This is the same investment vehicle I mentioned in the previous chapter. This type of account can also be setup in a child's name. While an IRA has penalties for withdrawals before fifty-nine and a half years of age, certain educational expenses can be withdrawn without penalty.

Uniform Gifts to Minors Act (UGMA) or Uniform Transfers to Minors Act (UTMA) – UGMA and UTMA are forms of tax-free savings accounts that allow minors to receive gifts and funds without having any tax consequences. Once the minor turns eighteen (sometimes twenty-one), these funds can be used for whatever the beneficiary chooses. Watch out on this one parents: The beneficiary can use these funds for whatever they want, while the other types of account, mentioned previously, restrict the money for educational expenses (unless they choose to pay heavy tax penalties).

Coverdell Education Savings Account – This account is similar to a 529 plan in that its contributions grow tax-free and can be withdrawn tax-free for educational expenses. Unlike a 529, contribution limits are smaller; however, expenses can be used for primary and secondary education, not just college and university. This is a great option for parents that want to enroll their children in private schools.

Traditional Savings Accounts – While you will not have tax benefits with a traditional savings account, it will allow you to earmark and set aside money for future educational needs in a simple manner that is connected to your other financial accounts. While tax-beneficial options are always better options, this category may be a good choice for individuals who are unsure about having children.

Choosing a Cost Effective School

If you are in high school and you are planning to attend college (or if you are the parent of a future college student), there are many other methods – outside of savings – that can reduce your tuition costs and loan needs. These methods are especially important for teenagers that will not have financial support from their parents, or for those that would like to reduce the financial burden on their parents. Whether you're a parent, a future college student, or a current college student, the options below will help you to reduce the amount of debt that you (or your child) take on.

Successfully reducing the cost of higher education often requires years of diligently saving, in addition to some early planning during high school. The first and most obvious option for reducing student loan debt is choosing the right school. Although it is not always possible (or desirable), it is important for high school students to determine what career paths interest them and stick to these paths as closely as possible. At the very least, a high school student that is unsure about his or her interests can choose a college that lends flexibility and lenience to changing majors. For instance, a college with fewer general requirements may provide the student with more time to complete a degree within an allotted four-year period, even if he or she has racked up credit hours that do not pertain to the new major. Too many young adults go to college just because they tell themselves, "It's what everyone does," and they do not have a plan; this can cost tens of thousands of dollars in wasted credit hours before they figure out new majors that appeal to their strengths and passions.

I would encourage students that are unsure about their future plans to attend community college. At nearly all community colleges, tuition costs are significantly cheaper than four-year universities; without the unnecessary financial pressure, community colleges offer a great venue to determine the area of study that most appeals to an undecided student. In my own home state of Tennessee, for example, residents are provided a free two-year technical or community college degree. After two years of community college, most universities allow transfer credits from community colleges. In this way, these students are able to graduate with a four-year degree (at the college of their choice) for a much lower price. This is a no-brainer for anyone that is uncertain about his or her educational needs and career path. Even for those that are sure of their career plans, a community college can provide half of a four-year education at a fraction of the price - simply by transferring from one school to another after two years. This is also a great option for students who need to get their grades and scores up before applying to four-year schools.

Another method in reducing future student loan payments is choosing a more COST-EFFECTIVE school. I use the verbiage "cost-effective" because the word "cheaper" has a negative connotation – though, no one's ever minded a cheap flight or a cheap date. Some of the best schools in the world can make for a lousy investment if you're paying outrageous tuition for a degree that will ultimately not pay off. On the other hand, you could choose a less expensive university that meets your educational needs and allows the same or better earning potential in the future (depending on the degree you choose). In-state school options also provide some of the most economical prices for education when it comes to quality. Even world-renowned state universities often have very affordable in-state tuitions. Consider these options first or consider establishing residency in a state for a year before entering college, rather than paying out-of-state tuition. This advance planning may save tens of thousands of dollars without having to compromise on your top school of choice.

When looking at school costs, it is important to look at Net Costs, which include all costs, such as tuition, room and board, books, supplies, etc. By law, colleges are required to publish these numbers; so, it is important to evaluate the total cost of attending a university rather than just looking at the cost of tuition. Another important consideration is financial aid, which could reduce the overall burden of loans a student has to take on. For example, if two universities have identical tuition costs, one may spend twice the amount per student on financial aid. Additionally, a small but rapidly growing group of universities have started a 'no loan' policy. (These are mostly prestigious schools with large endowments.) At these select schools, student loan requirements are kept to a minimum. This means that many of these top-notch universities have minimal tuition requirements and leave students with less than $10,000 of overall debt for a four-year degree, if they are accepted. Since many of these universities are the crème de la crème, it is important for high school students to get remarkable grades and test scores in order to become eligible for this rare type of opportunity.

Financial Aid, Scholarships, and Reducing Credit Requirements

The next opportunities to capitalize on are the following financial aid options: financial needs-based aid from the school, performance-based scholarships from the school, and independent scholarships. In almost every case, it is best to fill out a FAFSA and apply for financial aid. Many people automatically assume that they will not qualify for aid due to income limitations; however, you'd be surprised how often schools provide needs-based aid for students that didn't expect to qualify. In addition, being unqualified one year does not necessarily mean that you will remain unqualified the following year. It's best to get in the habit of filling out a FAFSA application, as your personal and familial financial situations may fluctuate without your knowledge. What's more is that you may be hit with unforeseen financial difficulties mid-way through the school year; and while schools can add students to aid packages after hardships, they can only do so in the event that the student has filled out the most recent FAFSA application on time. This is why it is critical to take the time to complete this form regardless of your financial situation. Wayne Gretzky once said, "You miss 100% of the shots you don't take." The same goes for student aid; you will not get anything that you do not ask for.

Outside of needs-based financial aid, there is also merit-based aid. Universities spend hundreds of millions of dollars in financial aid outside of need-based awards to incentivize top quality students to choose their universities. The better a student performs in terms of grades and scores, and the more well-rounded a student is, the higher the chance the student will qualify for merit-based aid. For example, I received over $10,000 a year in merit-based aid during my undergraduate studies, and then received a scholarship for 75% of the cost of my first master's degree - purely for my educational performance.

Remember that 'no' does not necessarily mean 'no' when it comes to student aid. When I first applied to my undergraduate university, I received a merit-based scholarship of $6,000 per year. I used the university's appeal process - which most schools have - to explain why I thought I deserved more based on my personal financial situation and my past academic performance. In taking this action, I was able to nearly double my annual scholarship to over $10,000 - just by spending a little extra time to explain my merits using the school's appeal process. Always spend the extra effort to apply. You never know how much more you can get until you ask!

Outside of school granted needs- and merit-based awards, prospective college attendees also have an (almost) unlimited number of local and national private grants and scholarships that they may apply to and receive aid from. Although the application processes can be tedious (just finding the most appropriate scholarships may take hours of effort!), the work can result in tens of thousands of dollars saved in student debt. These scholarships can be found both before and while enrolled at university. Be relentless in your search for opportunities. Depending on your educational aspirations, financial background, heritage, personal interests, etc., it is likely that you will find dozens of scholarships and grants that you are qualified for. You just have to do the research. Furthermore, many employers offer employees and their children tuition stipends and/or scholarships; so, make sure to start with employers (or your parents' employers). Use online resources, such as fastweb.com, to find hundreds of scholarships that meet your unique needs. I was able to get scholarships from IBM (my parents' employer), a local business competition, and a few other private scholarships. Combined, these reduced my loan requirements by over $5,000. There are plenty of opportunities out there; you just have to search for them!

So, what will help you seem more qualified than other scholarship applicants? One thing that will improve your chances of winning one or more of these scholarships is by earning high grades, both on report cards and on tests. Parents, encourage your children to excel through hard work so that they are eligible for these opportunities. Kids, listen to your parents - get good grades and diligently strive for perfect test scores. Work hard and it will make a huge impact on your life! Additionally, take as many AP classes as you qualify for in high school. The more

AP classes you pass, the less credit hours you will have to pay for in college. Even if tests and books are not your strong suit, there are a number of other ways you can earn scholarships. Thousands of talented athletes, musicians, writers, artists, mascots (seriously, big time D1 sports programs often give partial or full scholarships for being mascots!), and a ton of other passionate individuals earn partial or full scholarships from organizations or universities that value the skill sets these individuals have. If you have a passion, go after it! There is nothing quite as amazing as getting paid for something you enjoy doing. This will not only make a huge difference on the amount of loans you take out, but it will also improve your overall happiness in your professional life!

Choose Your Loans, Consider Future Salary & Reduce Debt While in School

At this point, you have nearly exhausted your options to reduce student loan debt. Now it becomes important to be realistic about salary expectations as they relate to the total burden of debt you will incur. Before enrolling in university, you should have a very good idea of what your total four-year student loan needs will be in order to cover tuition, room and board, and general expenses. Make sure that you are not signing up for an astronomical student loan burden that cannot be repaid by the salaries offered by your career choice. For example, if you are prepared to go into $200,000 of debt to become a highly-paid doctor, you will be able to pay off your debt if you simply follow the principles in this book. However, if you get into that same debt level for a degree that has very low salary expectations, you may want to reassess your choice of school and/or career; otherwise, you may be setting yourself up for a lifetime of debt that you cannot afford.

Finally, you are ready to begin applying for student loans. You should always begin this process by applying for federal government financial aid first. Federal financial aid (almost) always provides a lower interest rate loan, with more favorable terms than private banks. Only tap into private loans as a last resort when federal loans will not cover your entire education needs.

Remember, taking out loans does not equate to having "free money" for the length of your academic career. Even after you take out your loans, you should always try to reduce your current expenses in order to limit unwieldy student loan needs. At seventeen and eighteen years old, it is almost impossible to imagine making payments on something, nonstop, for ten years. All of the choices that you make once you set foot on campus will radically affect your loan burden after graduation. Simple choices like buying used books, living off campus, and working a job while studying will reduce your overall costs and increase your disposable income, which will ultimately reduce your overall student loan needs. Many schools offer work-study programs as part of financial aid packages; these types of programs allow you to work in a paid position (on campus or off). A few thousand dollars a year could be the difference between needing a loan or not, or not requiring a private loan in addition to a federal loan. Supplemental income can also be used to start paying off loans while in school or shorty after graduating. Remember, just because you don't have to start making loan payments yet doesn't mean that an unsubsidized loan isn't accruing harmful interest! The sooner you attack this debt, the better. If you do begin to make payments, either as the student or the parent of the student, make sure to take advantage of the American Opportunity Tax Credit. This program allows you to reduce your tax burden up to a certain threshold and within certain income limitations. Most importantly, once you graduate, follow the principles in the previous chapters to most efficiently eliminate your debt. By reducing your loan needs in the first place, you should be leaps and bounds ahead of the average graduate when Uncle Sam and private lenders come knocking on the door for repayment.

CONCLUSION

CONCLUSION

It is unfortunate that financial management courses are not required in most American high schools. Although we make major financial decisions at the end of our senior years in high school, most of us do not have the knowledge we need to ensure that these financial decisions are wise or feasible. After we graduate high school, it doesn't matter if we go to college, start our own businesses or simply want to buy homes – at the end of the day, we all need to know how money works and how to pay our bills to be successful. We can only do this by empowering ourselves to have financial freedom. Understanding and acting on the financial principles found in this book will make all the difference in eliminating student debt.

After (or nearly after) debt, you can continue to separate yourself from the average Joe by making wise financial decisions concerning investment opportunities. You now know how to budget and save, so use it to your advantage. Take the income you used to put aside for monthly loan payments and instead put that money to work for you. You can do this by researching and investing in a variety of retirement and non-retirement investment options. The preceding information is only a start; the more you can absorb, and the younger you come to improve your financial literacy, the higher the chance you have of sipping Mai Thais on a beach while your friends are working into their seventies, still saving for retirement. You will be traveling the world, enjoying your golden years, and having fun, instead of worrying about how you will ever be able to retire. At least, that is what my wife and I have planned for our future.

While my wife and I were busy paying off our student loans, I never planned on sharing our story. It wasn't until I reflected back on our missteps, good fortune, and the arsenal of parental and professional helpful advice we received that I realized the importance of packaging everything together and giving it to new graduates. The harsh reality is that many college graduates leave school with massive amounts of student debt, and almost none of us are prepared to spend tens of years repaying student loans. Despite the fact that student loan debt affects millions of young graduates, there are very few tools that help students and graduates take hold of their loan situations in an effective manner. It is my hope that this book and its contents will help you the same way it allowed my wife and me to eliminate student loan debt from our lives and become financially free.

ABOUT THE AUTHOR

Daniel J. Mendelson is originally from Vermont and currently resides with his wife in Memphis, TN. Before receiving his first professional job, Dan received a Bachelors and Master's in Biomedical Engineering from the University of Rochester and a Master's in business from the University of Memphis, which concluded a 7 year academic career on only $10,000 in student loan debt.

Daniel's wife, Meghan, did the exact same schooling and walked away with over **$110,000** in student loan debt! Together they had almost **$150,000** of debt **(including interest)**. By diligently following the principles outlined in this book, they eliminated all of their debt within five years of repayment. This provided the inspiration for this book – to help students get out of their student loan debt and gain financial freedom by sharing their story and simple steps to free students of their debt burden.